TRUST

A Story of Faith, Prep Sports, and Louisiana Politics

Lisa Arceri

WestBow
PRESS
A DIVISION OF THOMAS NELSON

WestBow Press books may be ordered through booksellers or by contacting:

WestBow Press
A Division of Thomas Nelson
1663 Liberty Drive
Bloomington, IN 47403
www.westbowpress.com
1-(866) 928-1240

Because of the dynamic nature of the Internet, any web addresses or links contained in this book may have changed since publication and may no longer be valid. The views expressed in this work are solely those of the author and do not necessarily reflect the views of the publisher, and the publisher hereby disclaims any responsibility for them.

Any people depicted in stock imagery provided by Thinkstock are models, and such images are being used for illustrative purposes only.

Certain stock imagery © Thinkstock.

ISBN: 978-1-4497-1497-0 (sc)
ISBN: 978-1-4497-1498-7 (e)

Library of Congress Control Number: 2011925894

Unless otherwise indicated, Bible quotations are taken from The King James Version of the Bible.

Printed in the United States of America

WestBow Press rev. date: 4/11/2011

This book is dedicated
to the purposes God has for it.

Contents

Chapter 1   I Am Sovereign; You Can Trust Me   1
Chapter 2   The Hard Part   9
Chapter 3   Starting with a Glass of Water   13
Chapter 4   Referred to the Committee on Education   19
Chapter 5   The Chairman   23
Chapter 6   HR 110 – The Study   29
Chapter 7   Lobbying Without Fear   35
Chapter 8   HB 531 – The 2009 General Session   41
Chapter 9   Chaos, Confusion, and Flying Amendments   47
Chapter 10   Relief   55
Chapter 11   The Baseball Bird   57
Chapter 12   HB 303 – The 2010 Session   59
Chapter 13   More about the Choice to Homeschool   75
Chapter 14   The New Law   83
Chapter 15   The Legislative Process   89

Chapter 1

I Am Sovereign; You Can Trust Me

Outside the Cenacle Retreat House

On June 29, 2010, Louisiana Governor Bobby Jindal signed legislation acknowledging the eligibility of homeschool athletes in Louisiana high schools. At the end of this book is the official history of this controversial legislation. This is our personal story behind that historical record. Many other stories could be told regarding this legislation. I have no doubt that God was at work through these same events in many more lives than our own.

This story is not only about educational choices, high school sports, and Louisiana politics. It is also about trusting that God knows all the details of our lives and is at work through all those details for our good.

My husband Chris and I both grew up in Louisiana. When our son Hozana was born, we had no idea that our choices about his education would lead to an experience with Louisiana politics. Life is certainly an adventure!

I knew before my children were of school age that I wanted to teach them at home. When the boys were young I was often asked, "So when will they go to school? How long will you homeschool?"

"As long as it's working for us," I'd reply. Homeschooling was working very well for our family, but as the high school years approached we knew there would be issues about athletics.

My oldest, Hozana, seemed wired to think about baseball. When I asked him for the sum of three and two, he immediately responded, "a full count." We were the neighbors that provided unwanted whiffle balls into back yards. The boys taught our dog to play the outfield and tag the runner. Hozana spray painted MLB team logos on the field (I mean the back yard).

My husband was much more aware of athletic issues than myself, and he contacted the LHSAA (Louisiana High School Athletic Association) years before Hozana would be in high school. After communicating with them, he was pretty sure they would not allow our sons to participate on a school team as homeschool athletes. In Jefferson Parish, competitive baseball after the age of fifteen is pretty limited to high school teams. There are some travel and showcase teams available, but those are usually more "off-season training" than the competition found in high school athletics.

So what were we to do? I believed that homeschooling in high school was a good thing for our family and for our sons, but the inaccessibility of high school sports created a fork in the road. It seemed we had to choose between sports and homeschooling. Many didn't understand why this was such a dilemma. Why wouldn't we just send them to school? No one suggested we tell them to just "hang up the cleats!"

Choosing to homeschool was not like choosing one curriculum over another, or one teaching method over another. Homeschooling was a choice of lifestyle, philosophy, and degree of involvement. It wasn't a choice of location or textbooks, but of how our family would live our lives. As well, in the current social and political culture, homeschooling seemed a necessity for us to pass on and reinforce the values and biblical worldview we wanted to teach our children.

My dilemma was the same as that of anyone who feels the pressure to make a decision against a conviction in their hearts. It's not very different than a high school student faced with peer pressure. What do you do when many around you are saying one thing and your heart says something else?

I learned early in my Christian walk that even an enormous pressure from without is much more bearable than the grief within caused by making a decision to relieve that pressure. God had taught me to think of my heart as strong, less moved by outward forces than by His Spirit within. I was always aware of the question, "Was I strong or just stubborn?" Sometimes it's hard to tell.

I needed direction from God and I needed to reflect on the situation. I wanted to do some soul searching. Most of all, I needed to hear from God on my situation. I didn't have much time to work with, so I called the Cenacle Retreat House to make a reservation for a couple of days of retreat. I became familiar with the Cenacle when I was in college, a time when I often took time off during breaks to seek God. The nice thing about the Cenacle was that it was so close to home; I didn't want to waste time traveling. I was able to arrange a couple of days on the weekend of my birthday. The retreat house is situated on Lake Pontchartrain, and as I sat watching the sun set the first evening, I was reminded of my first birthday as a Christian. I was a college student home from LSU. I remember being very aware that on that day when I was usually celebrating my natural birth, I was much more excited about my new birth as a believer. I drove out to Lakeshore Drive that day, and talked to people about Jesus. It was a wonderful day. I met people as I walked along the seawall, and made my way back walking along the levee on the other side. This journey concerning homeschooling and high school sports began on my birthday in 2006. Some of the biggest hurdles in the legislature happened on my birthday.

I don't know what other people do on retreats, but my intent was to meet with God. I started by getting a lot of thoughts and feelings off my chest and mind, discussing the situation with God and asking

Him to search my heart. One of the first things I reflected on was, "Why do I want to homeschool through high school?" It's a good thing in the presence of God to question oneself as well as encourage oneself in the Lord. I was quickly able to type out several pages of reasons I believed my sons should be homeschooled. I am not against traditional schooling, especially Christian schools which serve a vital function to society as a whole as well as to the individual students and families they serve. My concerns about traditional education for our own sons were not about how algebra and chemistry would be taught. It was about how much the social and political culture of our day would influence their hearts and minds through the educational and social experiences provided with that education. I knew these were critical years for young people, times when their focus could affect the next stages of their lives, when they would be making life-changing decisions. Was this the time to give up a large part of our influence as parents to an institution and to peers that may not be as concerned with the purposes of God in their lives? I know some may read this and think, "How ridiculous!" Many parents give up this influence even earlier. I'll discuss more about why I wanted to homeschool in a later chapter.

After reflecting on why I wanted to homeschool, I prayerfully submitted myself to whatever God wanted. Sometimes your will just has to override your heart. It's almost like taking the reins of a horse to direct it. I was just as determined to submit my will to God as I was to do what I thought was best. It was difficult knowing that my husband felt our only option was to send Hozana to school; that did appear to be the only option. I just kept thinking there was some way to do both, so I didn't want to choose between the two. I am one who believes unity is important in marriage, and knew that for my husband and I to walk as one, I had to be willing to send Hozana to school to play ball, if that was what Chris decided. I begged God to change my heart about the matter so I could be more supportive of a decision to enroll Hozana in school, if that's what it came to. I understood that if nothing changed, we had to make a decision, which meant choosing between homeschooling and sports.

Had both of us determined that homeschooling was more important, the situation would have ended with making that decision. Had both of us decided sports were more important, the situation would have ended with the boys in school. I was more unwilling to give up homeschooling, and Chris was more unwilling to give up sports for the boys. Our differences created a strong motivation to resolve the issue. I was willing to defer to Chris on the decision, and I thank God that Chris was just as willing to allow me to pursue changing the need for a decision.

I spent most of the remaining time of retreat worshipping the Lord, enjoying the quiet, and praying for friends. I was glad they put me away from the main part of the building in a room where I had a lot of privacy. I could sing and pray as loudly or quietly as I pleased not concerned about disturbing anyone. The night before I was to go home, I found myself in that quiet place of peace very aware of the presence of God. It's a place of worship where you don't want to move because of the pleasantness of His presence. This is what I had come for.

That's when God spoke to my heart. He said, "Lisa, I'm sovereign, and you can trust me." That was the answer I needed. It gave me great courage to go forward with whatever I would face, knowing I could trust Him. With that simple statement I gained so much strength. No matter what happened I would remind myself that God was in charge and I could trust Him.

God knew that day what would be before me, before I even thought about legislation. He knew this would take much longer than I expected. He knew those that would help, and those that would hinder. He knew Hozana would go to school briefly to play ball. He knew how much I would cry and how much I would laugh along the way. He knew what this would cost my family in time, effort, and resources. He knew how many people would be involved. How many people does it take to change a law to allow homeschoolers in Louisiana to play high school sports? How many legislators? How many staffers? How many families busy lobbying? How many saints busy praying? There were so many people who refreshed and encouraged us along the way. There were so many who wrote letters and sent emails, some who weren't even interested in sports. There were people who knew people who knew people who could help. There were those twelve pastors at the capitol the day we were heard in committee. There were family advocates who helped, and people who gave us lodging in Baton Rouge. There was the *God's Girls* breakfast group that covered us with prayer, my Mom who was always ready to help with laundry, and my sister Cherie who has a way of saying things that make you feel like you can do anything. It seemed every small part of the bigger plan involved so many different individuals, many that we could never have coordinated, but God was sovereign and could be trusted. He worked it all out perfectly, in His time.

It is such a good thing to have a personal relationship with One as powerful and mighty as God, who remains sovereign even though most are against Him, those to whom He gives the liberty and free will to be against or for Him. He remains in control without taking away man's liberty to choose. He knows the number of hairs on our head, the number of stars in the universe, and He can be trusted because He loves us.

Having been encouraged by the Lord in ways beyond what I knew at the time, I went straight from the Cenacle to a baseball game to meet Chris and the boys. Janet Burckel, a dear friend, was at the game and greeted me with a Birthday gift. How sweet. I sat in the hot, sweaty climate of a New Orleans summer and somehow knew that the path ahead would not be easy. I knew it would not be like sitting in the shade of a tree sipping lemonade. I knew it would probably be even more uncomfortable than the heat and humidity that day. I also knew that God was sovereign and that I could trust Him.

My story is one of being in places of difficulty, turning to God for help, and seeing Him, in all His sovereignty and wisdom, work things out well. It's a story of waiting on God, listening to His direction, and trusting that His will for us is good. It was not an easy path, but it was an even and straight one. It was sometimes difficult to believe things would go well when so much indicated otherwise, but it only takes a little faith in such a great God.

Being from the New Orleans area, I recall as a child looking at the carriages parked near Jackson Square as we walked home from a parade. Most of the horses wore a hat with holes cut out for their ears, the hat decorated with a fake flower. One of my fondest memories of my dad was walking along the street holding his hand, and raising our hands to clear the hitching posts that lined the street. I walked along the sidewalk, and he walked along the edge of the street. As we came to each pole, I'd raise my hand high, our grip clearing the pole. I can still see the horse head with the ring on its nose that sat atop the posts.

I asked once why the carriage horses had flaps besides their eyes. I was told the flaps were to prevent the horses from being startled or distracted by what passed by, staying focused on the road ahead. I felt like one of those horses at times. I needed blinders to focus on the path ahead of me. There were things I needed to ignore: words of discouragement, misunderstandings, disappointments, setbacks, defeats, and of course some of the laundry and housework I couldn't seem to get done as easily while I pursued this legislation. It was frustrating to see problems coming and yet not be able to do anything about it. We often had to stand by and watch conversations or testimony we were not given an opportunity to challenge. It was hard to watch, but I had the advantage of knowing God could be trusted. I had to remind myself that our fate was not in the hands of lawmakers, principals, or coaches, but in the strong arm of the Lord.

My story is much more about my adventure with God than the process of passing legislation, though we did learn a lot about politics and the legislative process along the way. Starting this with a reminder of God's sovereignty and trustworthiness was critical. Following is an excerpt from an email I sent out on June 16, 2010, after the bill passed:

> *After thanking some of the legislators and making a few phone calls, I headed home with a very grateful heart. When I called Arlene she cried (tears of joy). Getting on the interstate, I started to laugh - a happy laugh, praising God. I had a rush of memories*

of the many trials of going through this issue, and was very aware of how faithful God has been through it all. Years ago, before this legislation was initiated, I went away for a couple of days to seek the Lord about this issue and His words to me were, "I am sovereign, and you can trust me." As I praised God in my car today going home I could sense the Lord saying to me, "I said you could trust Me." and I sensed His pleasure. It is so good to know God and have His help in life.

Chapter 2

The Hard Part

A very difficult time for me began shortly after that retreat. God said I could trust Him. I must admit that I kind of hoped for some kind of miracle, and I had seriously considered moving to another state. Instead, we enrolled Hozana at a private school. Hozana had never been to school, and he started two weeks late because he was travelling with a Babe Ruth team representing Jefferson Parish. One morning I met some ladies who prayed for the school each day. They met on the bench outside the school office, and prayed for the students and the administration. These ladies were quite an encouragement to me in a difficult place.

Hozana did well in school, and enjoyed playing football, but before Thanksgiving we took him out believing there were too many issues that concerned us about him being there. That spring he umpired instead of playing ball, and I braced myself for what I knew would come the next fall. Again, we'd have to choose between homeschooling and sports.

My memories during this time are not as vivid, perhaps because they are not as fond. What I remember most is going before God with a troubled heart. Often I was without words in prayer; I simply cried. I felt like the depths of my soul were reaching desperately for wisdom and comfort. On the day we withdrew Hozana from school, he took longer than I expected to empty his locker. I asked him what took him so long, and he said he was looking for a pen.

He seemed hesitant to tell me why, but I curiously pressed him for an explanation. It was a personal thing, but he shared, "I left a note in my locker that said, 'I was a light in darkness.'"

There was a lot going on in our lives outside of this issue. My husband and I had started a Christian baseball league for youth about 5 years earlier, and we needed to get someone else to run that since our schedule was changing. As well, my husband's business was changing as a result of Hurricane Katrina. Educating three boys at home was enough to keep one busy; this entire ordeal was quite inconvenient.

In the fall, we enrolled Hozana in another private high school. It was hard for me to drop Hozana off each morning believing this was not the best for him, but I did the best I could to be supportive and make the most of the situation. This was a choice I didn't want to make. My gripe wasn't with the particular schools. They were among the best in the area. I met some very excellent teachers and administrators. Hozana had some teachers who really cared about their students, and were very good educators. I will try to explain later how it was not really about the academics, but about the environment. We wanted an environment that would best develop strength of character and Godliness in our sons' lives. Our experience with traditional school was not what we believed to be the best choice for our sons' education and development. It may work very well for many, but it wasn't for us.

I tried sending emails and letters to public officials about the issue, but got nowhere. Nothing was looking like we'd be able to homeschool AND give our sons the opportunity to play high school ball. I was already going in a direction I didn't want to go with my oldest son's education. What did the future hold for our other sons who were only a couple of years younger?

It's hard for someone who doesn't want to homeschool to understand why it would be such a big deal to choose between homeschooling and sports. If people understood how homeschooling was not only an academic choice but a lifestyle choice, they may perhaps understand why it would be so difficult to be put in the position to have to give up one or the other. Fortunately, I had some friends who weren't facing the same decision, but who were extremely supportive because they too valued their opportunity to educate their children at home. On Thursdays, my two younger sons and I went to a local playground to meet other homeschoolers for a PE class; Coach Dave had taught my boys PE since they were toddlers. Those ladies at PE were such a blessing. I recall one day when I was really struggling with Hozana being in school. As I walked up I think the ladies could see the discouragement on my face. Without asking any questions they kind of circled around me in a huddle and began to pray for me. I was strengthened by their prayers. As I walked away I realized it was a beautiful day with a comfortable breeze and a clear sky. It's amazing how the encouragement of friends can change our outlook on things. My youngest still goes to that PE class, and I'm blessed to enjoy the fellowship of some of the same women who encouraged me so much that year. God was in control, and I could trust Him. I trusted He was at work behind the scenes, but I was unaware of how.

I now know that there were a lot of people who had to be involved, and events that had to take place to work this out. Cameron Henry was one of those people, and his election as our State Representative was one of those events.

Chapter 3

Starting with a Glass of Water

Dot's Diner, where we had our first meeting with Representative Henry

I still remember the day Cameron Henry knocked on our door as he campaigned for State Representative. It was warm outside, and I invited him in for a glass of water. At the time I was very frustrated because we had to stop homeschooling my oldest son if he was to continue his interest in competitive baseball.

When I shared our dilemma with Cameron, he said that if elected he would propose legislation to address the issue. Not knowing Cameron, I didn't have high hopes that anything would happen, but I did vote for him and asked others to do the same. We'd have probably voted for Cameron anyway because he represented our general views on important issues. Would a politician keep a campaign promise? One made over a glass of water? I wasn't sure.

However, after he was elected, he carried this legislation for three years until it passed. I think most of us vote for representatives we hope will make decisions that go along with our general ideas of what's right or just. We characterize them along party lines, issues, or platforms, but rarely expect them to actually represent specific concerns which we think are important inLouisiana. I think it's easy to forget that they don't represent a party or political agenda, but a relatively small group of people in their political district. We are extremely grateful that Cameron carried legislation to address our concerns for Louisiana on this issue. I understood that this wasn't just a personal problem for my own family, but affected homeschool families across the state, and in a broader way was an issue about parental choice which I believe to be very important.

When I talked to Cameron that day I remember him say in regards to addressing the issue with legislation, "What could be so hard about that?" I don't think any of us had any idea just how hard it would be. Cameron may have been a new representative, but Arlene and I knew relatively nothing about the process. I think at times that was actually helpful. Being a bit naïve about things allowed us to be confident. We didn't know how much resistance there would be. We were usually unaware of the strategies that were working against us, but they were no match for Who was working for us.

I don't remember exactly how it came about, but Arlene Tafaro and I decided to get together to prepare for what would happen if Cameron kept his promise to propose legislation to address homeschool participation in LHSAA sports. Arlene and her husband, Craig, have become very good friends of our family in the past three years. We knew each other from a local homeschool group, and our sons liked hanging out together at the park on PE days. Her son, Tanner, and my boys got along well because they all liked sports. Tanner is about the age of my youngest son. He was a gymnast at a young age, but began to prefer football as he got older. Arlene also has a precious daughter, Riley, who is younger than the boys and is a spitting image of her mom. Riley loves to sing and is one of my favorites when it comes to singing the National Anthem at a ball game. When Arlene and I would get together to discuss legislation the boys were occupied shooting hoops, riding bikes, swimming or playing games. I could not have done this when my children were younger, and I can't imagine having done it without a friend like Arlene. Not only did the children get along well, but Arlene and I also worked well together as a team. This was probably because of our common concerns about homeschooling and athletics. We were both in the same boat; I had just been put out to sea first. Neither one of us could have done individually what we were able to do together. Our families were able to encourage each other. I have so many good memories of laughing with Arlene. She was good at finding humor in our circumstances.

We knew so little about the legislative process, but we were determined to learn. As homeschool moms we were accustomed to learning on the job. The first time we got together we talked about our goals, and divided up some of the research. We're not researchers, but we can *Google* and make phone calls as well as anyone else. Arlene had some contacts in other states that were going to give her information about similar efforts in Florida and Alabama. I was going to research the language of laws in other states that allowed homeschool participation in their state athletic association schools. We hoped to get information from the Department of Education and the LHSAA to better understand the facts. The Homeschool Legal Defense Association had already done some of this research; the information on their website was very helpful.

Arlene and I discussed how we wanted homeschool parents to have more choice regarding high school sports. We wanted to see unfair restrictions removed. We didn't want homeschoolers to have any unfair advantage or disadvantage; we just wanted a fair opportunity to participate. We determined two major criteria we would use to direct our involvement in legislative efforts:

1. Fairness and Equity that was reasonable.
2. No negative consequences to homeschoolers.

As we were getting started, I heard from Cameron's assistant, J.P., who wanted to set up a meeting for us to discuss the issue. Aware of deadlines approaching for legislation to be filed, we decided to show up at that meeting prepared with language we would recommend for the legislation.

We got together at Arlene's again. We noticed all the bills started and ended the same way, so that's where we began. Then, looking at language from other states, we began to put things together that applied well and fit with already established LHSAA policies and Louisiana law concerning homeschooling, continually checking to be sure it all fit our criteria. It's important to note that we didn't know if we were doing any of this the right way. I wondered if anyone would find our efforts a little too bold, but we decided it was better to express very specifically what we wanted than to leave it up to someone who may not understand the effects on homeschooling, or be committed to the same outcome. It was only by God's help and direction we had something to put in Cameron's hand at the meeting. We went through a lot of paper, and had notes scribbled all over the place, but I remember it seemed to come together easily. We would say it so many different ways looking for the right words, till we agreed, "That's it!"

When we met with Cameron and J.P. at Dot's Diner, we had in hand some specifics about what we wanted to see in the legislation, and were able to discuss some of our concerns. I realized at that meeting that one of our challenges would be the complexity of the issue. Cameron understood little about homeschooling, but he did have some experience with sports in high school. The issue involved LHSAA rules, homeschool law, principals, districts, private and public schools, fairness issues, a variety of interested parties, etc. Arlene and I were focused on the details of the issue, not realizing that this was going to be as much about politics as it was about baseball.

I was kind of oblivious to that, thinking we just had to write legislation that covered everyone's concerns fairly, and voila! – Problem solved. It wasn't so simple. We had no idea what we were getting into, unprepared but willing to learn, driven by the passion that is common to moms who want the best for their children. At first, we didn't really embrace the political reality of the situation. It took a long time for us to "get it" and understand that passing this particular legislation involved emotions, philosophies, and ideas as much as a simple statement of facts. It was a power struggle, a strategy, and a maneuvering behind the scenes, all things unfamiliar to Arlene and me. Yet, as Paul said to the Romans, "If God be for us, who can be against us?" God was very faithful to lead us and give us favor in a very humbling and sometimes intimidating experience. He could be trusted.

Chapter 4

Referred to the Committee on Education

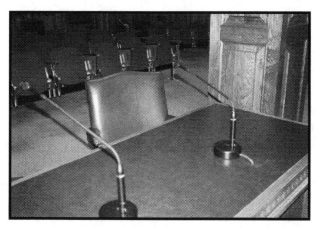

We sat before the sixteen members
giving a statement, and answering questions.

We had a lot of "Oh, I didn't know that" moments going through all this. The first of these was learning that there were legislative analysts and staff that assisted the legislators with writing bills. (I thought Cameron was going to write it.) Cameron gave one of those analysts permission to discuss the language with us before the bill was filed. Looking back, this was extremely important. Conversations with him made us aware of parts of the bill that would be debated, and helped us see the need for clarification in certain areas. More importantly, our involvement assured our input to keep it on a track that was consistent with our intentions. I was very impressed by how professional and capable the Education Committee analysts were. They were also very gracious about answering our many questions about the process, questions which probably revealed how little we knew.

Arlene and I had put effort into what we thought was the hard part, the language of the bill. Little did we know; that was the easy part. We got pretty excited when we saw the bill posted on-line with a bill number (HB 871). To us each step seemed monumental. We didn't realize that HB 871 (House Bill 871) would have a short life span.

We were a bit puzzled when we were told we didn't need to come to the Committee Meeting. We not only wanted to come, but expected to make a statement, and hoped the bill would pass through the committee. On the morning of the meeting, a call was placed to tell us not to come, but we missed the call and were on our way. We realized when we heard the voice mail about not coming that things were not going as we expected. It seemed as though everything had been decided before we even showed up.

In the elevator, we ran into a lobbyist that was a friend of my sister. I told him I was concerned the Chairman of the Committee may want the bill deferred or sent to study. He mentioned that we may want to suggest it be voluntarily deferred so we could come back after more discussion with legislators. Many were unaware that Governor Jindal was supporting the legislation. Arlene and I knew he was supporting the legislation, but we didn't realize the Governor was involved in the process. Another "Oh, I didn't know that" moment. I now know that the support of the Governor can be very important. I don't think anyone expected the bill to be debated, but we did get our first opportunity to discuss the issue with legislators on the Committee.

It was the first time Arlene and I had attended a Committee meeting, no less made a statement. We were fairly nervous, but once into the discussion I felt more relaxed and comfortable answering questions. We were well prepared and none of the questions were very hard to answer if one understood the issues. The representatives are apparently only supposed to ask questions, but when they wanted to make a comment they simply tagged "did ya know?" to the end of the statement. For the first time we were able to publicly hear some of the objections to the idea of our children participating in high school sports.

Right off the bat one of the representatives asked the question which was a favorite talking point of our opposition, "If the schools are not good enough for homeschoolers, why is the athletic program?" First of all, there's a big "IF" in this question. It assumes we don't think the schools are good enough, and sounds defensive about it. We emphasized that we never said the schools weren't good enough. We had our own reasons for homeschooling which we didn't think should be a part of the debate.

This same question came up on a local radio talk show. One of the House Education Committee members was on the line and asked the question. The host responded by asking him if the coaches were better than the math teachers. His answer was that the coaches also taught in the classroom. Then, the host asked if they were perhaps better at coaching. The host turned the "If" assumption of the question into a question of his own. The question of the adequacy of public education is not a question relative to homeschool participation in athletics. Obviously, for whatever reason, and I would say it is not usually a matter of how a certain subject is taught, some families believe it would be better for them to educate their children at home. So the question should be more about if it would be feasible and reasonable to allow their participation in athletics, than about a comparison of the two choices regarding academic superiority. The question is divisive, assuming homeschoolers see traditional schooling as inferior, which is not the case.

In the meeting, one of the representatives commented, "We don't know what they (homeschoolers) are doing during the day. Did ya know?" Did she need to know? The homeschoolers we were addressing in this legislation were already verifying the adequacy of their education by standardized tests or reports from certified teachers. Was it that we educated our children in the privacy of our home that bothered her? We are a free people with rights to privacy. Did she feel the rearing of our children or their education should not be at our own discretion, but under the watchful eye and control of the state? I don't think I understood her question.

We did have some kind comments from some of the representatives. Based on the number of homeschoolers and the cost of public education per student, one of the representatives calculated that Louisiana homeschoolers were saving tax-payers $64,000,000 in education costs. Unfortunately, there are some who see our taking financial responsibility for our children's education not as saving tax-payer funds, but as taking money out of the system.

When finished, we went to the back of the room. Representative Henry explained that he didn't know how people would vote, and that the chairman wanted to send the bill to study. We talked about having it voluntarily deferred, and he left the decision up to us. We chose to have it come back after we could speak more with legislators. While we were chatting, the LHSAA and a few principals were testifying to the Committee in opposition to the bill. In Representative Henry's closing, he asked for the bill to be voluntarily deferred, and it was. HB 871 wasn't dead yet. God was still at work, and could be trusted.

Chapter 5

The Chairman

The garden porch outside the capitol,
where Arlene and I went after meeting the Chairman

Leading up to this first Committee meeting, Arlene and I did not understand the concept of lobbying. We thought it was just a matter of answering the legislator's concerns in the committee meeting. We didn't know what to think after the meeting; we were told the bill would be rescheduled. As time passed we realized that the Committee Chairman did not want to reschedule the bill for a vote. Our efforts to reach him were not very successful. Finally, after frequently calling his office, he agreed to a meeting.

We knew going into the meeting that he was against the legislation. We felt that might change if we had the opportunity to address his concerns and discuss the matter with him. He didn't ask questions in the committee meeting, and we didn't really know where he was coming from. We met one morning in his office. His demeanor and tone were very non-threatening, but his words were otherwise. After a bit of conversation he said that we didn't know what or who we were messing with, and that we better back off. He promised us that it would be handled the next year, and asked us to trust him. I remember looking at Arlene and seeing an expression that seemed to mirror what I was thinking, "What???"

I asked the chairman, "And how can you promise that? Do you have that kind of authority and influence?" To our shock, he believed he did, or at least expected us to believe it. I asked him if he could put his promises in writing. He even got someone from the LHSAA on the phone to tell us that if we'd back off, they would show us how to get eligibility for our sons and put us on one of their committees to work this out. We weren't interested in being on some committee that wouldn't do what we had come to the Education Committee to do. It appeared as if they thought we'd be thrilled to be on a committee of some kind. I did actually receive a letter from the LHSAA promising to put us on a committee, which would not have made any difference. Being on a committee wasn't the promise we were interested in. They didn't even keep the promise about the committee. The deadline they set for it in the letter came and went. However, more than a year later the LHSAA did invite us to their office to discuss the issue.

After leaving the meeting with the chairman, we sat in the garden outside the capitol and looked at each other shocked. "Was he trying to threaten us?" Arlene asked. We didn't know what to think. I'd been caught smuggling scriptures into the Soviet Union in the early eighties, and had dealt with the KGB. I certainly wasn't intimidated by a politician eating a muffin trying to dissuade us.

The Chairman succeeded in being a wall that stood in our way that first year. He would not allow the bill to be heard unless it was agreed that it would be sent to study. After we did all we knew to do, we found out after the fact that it had been sent to study. Talk about an "I didn't know that" moment; I didn't even realize the bill was dead. I thought it went to study, as if it would come out of study after it was studied. No, HB 871 was most certainly dead, but we weren't ready to give up. If anything, in the process to this point we became aware of other families in Louisiana who faced the same choices we were facing, which only motivated us more to do something about it.

Throughout the process we often realized that we were not aware of what was really going on behind the scenes. As well, we could sometimes tell when someone wasn't being honest with us, but we didn't know exactly how. We were in a political environment where there were a lot of different agendas at work. For some, accomplishing one thing might be at the expense of another. There may have been some who didn't even care about the effect this had on us personally. But God knew everything going on behind the scenes. Nothing was hidden from Him, and He would work things out well as we trusted Him.

We had been told that if we backed off from the legislation the LHSAA would show us how to obtain athletic eligibility. We had no intention of backing off, but I did want to find a way for Hozana to play ball as a homeschool athlete.

The LHSAA did have a rule for homeschool participation. The problem was that the rule was vague and inapplicable. Most schools would not consider taking the risk since reading the rule implied that the student must be enrolled in the school, that their grades must be on the school's transcript, and that those grades must be approved by the Louisiana Department of Education (LDE). Enrolled in the school? For a public school in Louisiana, enrollment meant MFP money. Why would the school's transcript include the homeschool's grades? Some principals thought this meant they would have to give the student credit for courses they finished at home. Approved by the LDE? What they meant was that the student must be in a home study program approved by BESE, but that's not what the policy said, it's not what the principals were told, and it wasn't the case with the few homeschool athletes who were participating according to the rule. There was risk associated with having an ineligible player, not a risk most principals wanted to entertain with so many details unclear.

In defense of some of the LHSAA leaders, I think there were some who recognized the need to clarify their policy, but just as many who wanted to do away with it completely. I was often asked, "Who is it that is so against homeschool participation in high school sports?" The LHSAA said it was the principals. The principals said it was the LHSAA. Since principals make up the LHSAA, maybe both were right. The LHSAA said publicly that they already allowed homeschool participation. They said homeschoolers can't or don't want to go through the process to qualify; that was not the case. The truth was that there was no clearly defined rule or process for homeschool athletes or principals to follow regarding homeschool participation.

Cameron said we could try again next year. Waiting a year was 25 percent of the time Hozana would be in high school. The Bible teaches that hope deferred makes the heart sick, but desire fulfilled is a tree of life. Going back to "I am Sovereign; you can trust Me" made me realize that even if having a choice was being deferred at least a year, my hope need not be deferred. I could still trust that God would work this out in His time and in His way.

Considering the path may be a longer one than I'd hoped, I encouraged myself in the Lord. No one likes to wait, but waiting on the Lord is a good thing. I thought of Dmitri Mendeleev's mom. Most know that Mendeleev invented the Periodic Table of Elements, but many don't know about his mom. My children and I read about her in a Chemistry book. Dmitri was the youngest of seventeen children living in Tobolsk, Siberia, in Russia. Dmitri's mom had to support the family after her husband became blind; he died when Dmitri was thirteen years old. Dmitri loved Math and Science, and his mom moved 1,500 miles to enroll him in the University of Moscow. He was not admitted to the University because he was a Siberian. She then took him to St. Petersburg, another 500 miles away, where he was also turned away. At the time it was believed that Siberians would not make good students. Mendeleev faced his share of discrimination, but with his mom's persistence, he eventually became a faculty member at one of the Universities that had denied his admission. I could relate to this woman's heart. She just wanted to do what was necessary to make it possible for her son to pursue his interest, which for Dmitry was science.

Most parents can relate to this desire to provide the best opportunities available for their children, and when not available, to try to make them available. If there are families in Louisiana that believe homeschooling is the best choice for their sons or daughters, then why should an interest in high school sports prevent that choice? Surely this needed to be pursued further.

House Resolution 110 was the request for BESE to study the issue, a request initiated by HB 871 going before the House Education Committee. The study was supposed to only take a few months, but we were dealing with the study and its findings into the next Legislative session. We were trying to follow the study at the same time that we were planning for the next session, in our free time. There were so many reasons to doubt this was working, but God could be trusted to work it out well.

Chapter 6

HR 110 – The Study

*The Louisiana Department of Education
is in this building, behind the capitol.*

We were still pretty confused about what was next with these legislative efforts, but by the end of the summer we did decide to homeschool Hozana again. We hoped to find a principal who would work with us in pursuing Commissioner Henderson's interpretation of the LHSAA homeschool policy. Hozana played what would be the last competitive year available in the Jefferson Parish Summer League, and signed up to play in a fall, off season league for high school players.

Meanwhile, "The Study," House Resolution 110, was in the hands of The Board of Elementary and Secondary Education (BESE). We didn't really understand the process; we were only aware that

BESE would report the results of the study to the Legislature the next session.

We were contacted in August about coming to a meeting at the Louisiana Department of Education (LDE) concerning the Resolution. That meeting went well despite the fact that we were contacted about the meeting the day before it was to take place. It was inconvenient to make arrangements to go to Baton Rouge at the last minute, but we were not about to miss it. There were just three homeschool moms and three ladies from the LDE there at the meeting. They told us their plans for a survey of the principals, and shared with us some of what they had found so far. There were three questions on the survey designed to discover concerns the principals had about homeschool participation in high school sports. We were told that the third question was designed to determine if the principal's resistance to the idea wasn't based on the concerns they had expressed. The third question asked if they would support homeschool access if all their noted concerns were addressed, and policies were budget-neutral.

We indirectly received an email which made us aware of what was going on with the survey. The email was from the LHSAA to their member principals. We called the LHSAA to verify that the email was from them and was legitimate. Their secretary confirmed that it was. The email was in its own words, "Urgent!" because only 67 of the 395 principals had responded to the survey. The email warned the principals that they must respond to prevent the legislation. The attempt by the LHSAA to influence the results of the survey seemed inappropriate in a study requested by the Legislature. As well, anyone who has done research or studied statistics knows that non-response cannot be ignored in an outcome.

While we were working on preparations for the Legislative Session, someone sent us an email letting us know of the report that the Board was to discuss for approval at their next meeting. Arlene and I knew so little about the Department of Education, probably less than we knew about the workings of the Legislature, but we were ready to learn.

Following is the conclusion of the study that BESE was to discuss for approval:

> *In consultation with the Louisiana High School Athletic Association (LHSAA), it has been determined that guidelines, procedures, and standards that address existing barriers and which are also directly related to participation in the activities sponsored by the association, lay outside the current scope of state responsibility. After an initial review of the LHSAA guidelines for homeschool student participation, collaboration with homeschool associations to identify barriers and recommend solutions, survey results from public and nonpublic school representatives, and a review of other sources of information, the State Board of Elementary and Secondary Education recommends to the House and Senate Education Committees that the issue of participation in interscholastic athletics be resolved collaboratively between the LHSAA participating school and the LHSAA in the manner deemed most appropriate through that partnership.*

> *- Executive summary, HR110 report*

We of course disagreed not only with this summary report, but also with the way it came to be. The summary basically said that the LHSAA should collaborate with itself about the matter and that the state should stay out of it. Who came up with that? The report ignored its own findings, and allowed the LHSAA undue influence. Though there was some effort to reach out to homeschoolers, it was hardly the collaboration and consultation with stakeholders set out in the Legislative Action Plan. I gave up trying to find out who actually wrote this summary. The best I could find out was that the LHSAA was very involved in the recommendations.

The findings were based on a survey that was conducted with bias; how could the results have been unbiased? The survey findings indicated that the survey went to over 200 principals. It actually went to over 300 and closer to 400, which is significant when interpreting any percentages of the total considering non-response. Only 67 of the 209 that responded were not potentially influenced by the LHSAA's email. Besides the inappropriateness of their influence, that's an effect on about 60 percent of the survey responses and leaves the possibility that apart from outside influence more than 80 percent might not be overly concerned, which may explain why only a handful of principals ever came to the committee meetings. The survey report stated that the reason 162 of 194 principals would not support homeschool access even if all their noted concerns were addressed was because of "widely held views that a school team involves more than student participation in athletic events." However, the survey responses did not indicate that reason based on the responses to Question three, but instead indicated reasons that have to do with perceptions of homeschooling in general, and misunderstandings of the proposed legislation. We thought the survey provided unreliable information that should not have weighed so heavily on the report.

We also disagreed with the conclusion that the proposed legislation was outside the current scope of the State. The LDE, the LHSAA, BESE and the Legislature should all be interested in facilitating understanding and equal opportunity in the community to all students, and discourage unwarranted discrimination against any particular population of those students, including those who are educated at home. According to the Louisiana constitution, the department should provide equal opportunities for all individuals to maximize their full potential. This decision should not have been about the preference of the LHSAA or the preference of Homeschool associations or students. It should have been about BESE making an informed recommendation that is right and reasonable for high school students in Louisiana. The LHSAA had already been given opportunities to change its policy, and was unable or unwilling to do so.

Like so many other things, we had to learn along the way. We assumed if there was a public hearing, we could go, and make comment. We did. It was quite awkward, and very frustrating to not know what we should or shouldn't say. At one point one of the

Board members told me to quit while I was ahead. I had no idea what he was talking about, but we shut up, and the Board deferred House Resolution 110. No report was better for us than the report that had been written.

By this time BESE had begun to review bills for the upcoming 2009 session. There were individuals in the Department of Education, and individual members of BESE who sided with the LHSAA or who opposed homeschool participation in high school athletic programs. Most though recognized the need to have good policy on the issue. By the 2010 session, the LDE and BESE publicly supported the legislation. No doubt the Governor's agenda helped solidify this support.

At this point we began to understand how to read schedules, follow things on line, and even began to recognize some of the legislators and board members. During the upcoming session we would learn how to talk to legislators, which would change how we approached the process.

Chapter 7

Lobbying Without Fear

*The entrance into one of the committee room halls,
a favorite place to talk to lawmakers*

Early on in this process a friend, Suzanne, gave me a phone number for Jerrie LeDoux. She said Jerrie might be able to help us with all this. Jerrie was more than a help; she and her daughter Morgan were a Godsend. The first time I spoke to Jerrie she rattled off the names of about seventeen people I should call. Problem was I didn't know what to say when I called them. I tried to make a few calls, but didn't know where to go with the conversations. I couldn't say, "I don't know you, you don't know me, but I need your help." That was about all I knew. One of the first people I called was trying to talk me out of pursuing legislation. It wasn't till I met Jerrie in Baton Rouge one day that I figured out what she meant by talking to Legislators. To this day I find it very difficult to initiate phone conversations, but Jerrie helped us understand how to talk to legislators at the capitol.

Jerrie was working on the Dual Enrollment Bill, legislation that would allow homeschool students to participate in a program that allowed Louisiana high school students to take courses at Louisiana colleges and universities. I watched as she walked the halls of the capitol talking to legislators. It was another one of those "I didn't know that" moments. I remember standing at the end of one of the committee room halls thinking, "Oh! We need to speak with the legislators about the bill, and we can do that here!" I was beginning to understand what everyone else in the building probably knew already, that votes passed bills, and communication with legislators was part of getting those votes. For some reason, I pictured each of these representatives having an office at the capitol, and that talking to them would require appointments; we'd already been quite unsuccessful getting a phone call returned or an appointment set up. I learned that their office was usually the Chamber where they had a desk and a computer, a space where only representatives were allowed and where hand-written messages could be delivered.

At first I found it hard to figure out who was who, even with the PAR guide Jerrie had given me. The Public Affairs Research (PAR) Council of Louisiana publishes a guide to the Legislature that includes photos of lawmakers, seating charts, committee members and other information an active citizen might need at the capitol. Over time I became more familiar with their faces, especially after I began to pray for them. I used their pictures to remind me to pray. We actually had the Education committee members' pictures posted in our hall and on our refrigerator door to remind us to pray for them. I began to see them not as a vote I needed but as a person, a husband, a wife, a mom or dad. I realized their lives were much more than being a lawmaker. Even those who were almost hostile to our cause, when I prayed for them, I saw them differently.

Going to the capitol was outside of my comfort zone. I was used to grocery stores, playgrounds, churches and museums. I was used to chatting with women about Christian doctrine, recipes, teaching methods, and child discipline. I didn't own professional attire, and wasn't into small talk. The legislature is made up mostly of men, men with power. Being a woman, a mom, an ordinary citizen not representing any association or organization was a little intimidating, but I was not one to be thwarted easily by fear. Knowing who we are in Christ dispels many fears of others. When I began a relationship with God through Jesus Christ, I became connected with the One who had created the heavens and the earth. I have a friend in much higher places than the highest seats in government. Respect is due offices and positions, but fear will stifle any efforts to petition the government and its leaders.

When I lived in Hattiesburg, a student at the University of Southern Mississippi, I worked as a waitress on a nearby military base. I remember the first time a General showed up for lunch at The Officer's Club. There was a flurry of activity in the kitchen and everyone was nervous. Baffled by the panic, I told one of the waitresses, "He may be a general, but he's still just a man who wants lunch." She asked me to take his table since I was so at ease with the situation. I thought to myself, "Fine. I'm sure he and his aids probably tip well, too."

I always treated the officers with respect, and said to myself as I walked to his table, "Lisa, treat him the same as you would any other officer." I did. After the meal I told him I was an ambassador, and wanted to know what rank an ambassador has. He told me an ambassador was a high ranking official, and he gave me a hat with a star on it like his. He asked me how I was an ambassador, and I explained how I was an ambassador for Christ to this world. He thanked me for serving him, and yes, left a good tip. The encounter, like others in my life, reminded me that no matter how important people are, or how much authority they have, there is no need to fear approaching them. The General had come into the restaurant making it necessary to talk to him, whereas talking to legislators required initiating a conversation from nowhere which was more difficult. Legislators usually looked very busy and had a lot of people waiting to speak to them. At times, we felt like we were imposing on them to initiate a conversation.

Going to the capitol, even if we were not afraid, was still awkward. I felt like a fish out of water sometimes. There was so much we didn't know; we didn't even know the right questions to ask. I called representatives senators, and senators representatives. I called some by the wrong name (they didn't look like their picture), and I would often knock over their name plates when I extended my hand to meet them after a committee meeting. Jumping into this without already understanding how the process works made us especially prone to a capitol faux pas here and there.

It was a bit of a balancing act. On one hand, we had to be bold to get things done, but on the other hand, we were very aware of how little we knew. In most circumstances, inexperience calls for taking a step back and observing, but this situation required us to speak without being timid. I remember praying silently as I approached one of the lawmakers, "Oh God, please help me not say something laughable or unintentionally offensive." I soon realized that once we got past the introductions, God would give us words and direction in conversations.

Once we were around the capitol a few times we noticed several different groups of people. There were the legislators, easy to spot by the pin on their lapel if we didn't already recognize their faces from our PAR guide. Then there were the paid lobbyists, dressed very similar to the lawmakers, but wearing a red ID badge. They were the ones that looked like they knew everyone. The Sergeants at Arms were obvious in their maroon blazers, and the aids and pages were the young ones also wearing IDs. Staffers were easy to spot because they were usually carrying around files, obviously on their way to another floor or office. Like us, there were the "people" coming to the "people's" house, some obviously students or tourists. The citizen activists usually wore their agendas on their shirts or on a sign. They wore buttons and traveled in groups wearing the same color. Then there were citizens obviously affected by legislation, seen circled around a legislator in a hallway as he explained the plan or outcome of a vote. These were the people with concern on their faces, whose lives were obviously being impacted by votes on a bill. My heart went out to them; I could relate.

One of the first times I got on the elevator near the cafeteria I met a woman whose kindness and smile I will not forget. She had an armload of files and smiled at me as she pushed the button for her floor. Perhaps she could tell I was new to the place and involved with trying to pass legislation. She smiled at me and said, "Hang in there; it takes time. Keep trying." Now this was someone I met in the elevator, hardly a friend, not even an acquaintance. Yet I felt I had made a friend in what at the time seemed an unfriendly place to my cause. I was encouraged. It wasn't the first time she'd encourage me with her kindness.

Believing we didn't have time for homeschool parents to feel comfortable initiating conversations with legislators, we decided to produce some props which would also serve as a reminder to the lawmakers of our conversations with them. In the 2009 session we put together a booklet that we could refer to about the issue and leave with lawmakers. It also made it easier to begin a conversation after introductions by asking, "Did you get this booklet yet?" Using different pieces of literature or items each time we went to the capitol allowed us to feel comfortable talking numerous times to certain lawmakers. I doubt many read everything we gave them, but it was a prop in conversation, and at least made them aware there was a discussion of the issue available. We realized that it may take several different conversations before they might begin to think more about the issue. Sometimes it felt like we were just trying to get their attention, and help them understand who we were and what we represented. We tried to tackle a different concern or aspect of the legislation on each visit.

Our children were with us on many visits. We tried to coordinate the trips to the capitol with field trips to the many educational opportunities in Baton Rouge. I think the boys liked the USS Kidd the best, and of course going to the observation deck atop the capitol almost every time we were there. The boys started to know their way around, and became more familiar with the people in the capitol. I found my sons better at recognizing faces than myself. I'd often say, "Who's that?" and they knew. They were good at using the capitol computers to find out who would be in what committee, when, and what bills were being debated. They also figured out what they liked best for lunch at the cafeteria, muffuletta and fries; I liked the fish. Having them walk through some of this with us was a much better way for them to learn the legislative process than reading it in a textbook. None of my sons are currently interested in politics or government, but this was a great way to enhance their Civics curriculum.

God was at work; He knew this would take longer than we expected. Perhaps God sometimes took us the long way to build faith in our hearts. With each step that revealed His faithfulness, we were more prepared to trust Him.

Chapter 8

HB 531 – The 2009 General Session

The entrance to the Louisiana State Capitol

We met with Cameron over the holidays between Christmas and the New Year. We discussed what had happened in 2008, and ways to avoid the same problems in 2009. Cameron had a year of experience behind him, hopefully preparing him for what the LHSAA might do behind the scenes.

Other families from around the state got involved. There were some families that we looked forward to seeing at the capitol, not just for help with the legislation, but for the fellowship we enjoyed with them. People drove far distances to be there, and I always wished we would have had more time to just visit with each other. There were people I emailed and spoken with on the phone, that I never met, but to whom I was very grateful. Our efforts were not extremely coordinated as we had very limited resources and means of communicating with homeschoolers across the state. About all we had time for was to send information to a handful of contacts hoping they would get the word to others. Homeschoolers have layers of networks, which would go into action if homeschooling were threatened in Louisiana. There are local, state, and national associations that would be mobilized if that were the case. However, this issue was of specific concern to Louisiana homeschool families who were interested in competitive high school athletics, a relatively small number of families. We actually had more support than we expected, support that went beyond that small number of families.

Liz Champagne and her family from Lafayette were extremely helpful. She and her boys talked to legislators numerous times at the capitol, and helped us in planning. Liz is a very petite woman, but there's nothing petite about her heart and determination. Pastor Rick Aultman, his wife Jean, and their children also helped on numerous occasions driving all the way from Mangham, Louisiana. The Aultman's oldest son, Nathan, was Hozana's age. John Burke from New Orleans was also very helpful, especially considering he was involved in efforts to coordinate a homeschool football team. He realized that what he was doing was not currently available in most communities around the state, and did not provide an opportunity for all sports outside of football. I appreciated that John didn't feel threatened by what we were doing. As he put it, "I just think parents should have as many choices as possible." God had brought us together from across the state to stand together on this issue.

We had a lot going on in our lives: educating our children, taking care of our husbands and families, cooking, cleaning, ball games, music lessons, field trips, dentist appointments, Science fairs, hatching chickens, etc. I tend to be an organizer, and knew our efforts weren't being very well planned. We had to trust that God was at work in ways we couldn't have planned. One day I received a call from a mom I'd never met. She was talking to legislators at the capitol about the bill, and had some questions for me. We also had people show up at committee meetings that we'd never met. Little things like that reminded us that God was at work behind the scenes doing so much more than we were able.

In 2009 we had the "football" which turned out to be very helpful. Our theme was "Sign the Ball – Pass the Bill." Arlene lives down the street from one of the New Orleans Saints, who agreed to be our first signature on the football. Written on the ball was, "Let'm play" and we wanted to get the signatures of legislators who were supporting the bill. This was an idea that we hoped would help us initiate conversations and that would get the attention of some of the lawmakers. We were a bit nervous about asking lawmakers to sign our football, until we met with a former LSU football coach who taught a Sunday school class I attended while a student at LSU. He signed the ball and told Arlene and I that we didn't need to be so "nice." He said we needed to be "tough." He said, "Is what you're doing important? Is it valuable? If it is, then it's worth fighting for." We didn't know exactly what to do with the "don't be so nice" advice, but his words, "It's worth fighting for," gave us courage to not back down.

When legislators expressed support for the bill, we asked them to sign the ball with their district number. Legislators seemed less willing to say so if they were against the legislation, but their not wanting to sign the ball helped us know they were truly undecided or against the bill. Now we had some direction. We would continue to say hello and thank lawmakers who had signed the ball, and we wanted to hear the concerns of those who didn't sign it. If we found their objections to be political or involving a bias against homeschooling, we spent less time talking to them, not believing our conversations would make much difference. When we saw them at the capitol we tried to be more lighthearted, acknowledging that we understood their opposition and appreciated their public service even if they didn't support the bill. We tried to avoid arguments though there were a few with whom discussions could become quite animated. We used the ball as our checklist for who was for the bill, and who we still needed to talk to about their concerns. We found out that one of the Sergeant at Arms had played professional football, and asked him to sign the ball, too. The boys looked forward to seeing him to talk sports. It was pretty exciting to see the ball filling up with signatures. It was also a good way for lawmakers to see which of their colleagues were supporting us.

On my birthday in 2009, HB 531 made it through the Education Committee, our first real victory in the process. It was a close vote, and I don't think anyone knew who would vote how. I remember Cameron looking down at his tablet making marks as the votes were called out. I think there were a lot of people rooting for our success, but with that victory came more opposition.

When the bill went to the full house for debate, we faced last minute amendments by a particular representative. We knew the amendments were bad, but in the pressure of the moment it was hard to get anyone to really listen to our concerns. We usually referred to the amendment by the name of the legislator who proposed it, but for the purposes in this book I'll call it the "public/private amendment" because it scrambled the language regarding public and private schools. Changing the word extracurricular activities to athletic activities was a good clarification made by the amendment, but taking out the word "public" to make the bill apply to non-public schools was a big problem. For one thing, the intention was not to improve the bill, but to give it trouble. An application for non-public schools was already addressed in the bill in a way that allowed them to have homeschoolers participate. Most of the bill intentionally addressed public schools, and to change those parts gave some the impression we wanted to force private schools to allow our participation, which could not have been further from the truth. I suspected that the "public/private amendment" was well thought out beforehand to appear like a good thing. We were the last to hear about it.

The "public/private" amendment was just the beginning of opposition on the House floor. There was a motion to table the bill; that motion failed. There was an attempt to amend another bill into the bill; that also failed. After a lengthy debate, the bill passed the House. There were a couple of representatives who were quite vocal about their opposition. I don't think they realized that their ranting against us often brought us more support. There were a lot more important issues to discuss in the capitol, but homeschooling issues usually drew lengthy, emotional debates. We knew we had the votes in the house, but were very disappointed that the "public/private amendment" would force us to make changes in the Senate which would then make it necessary to return again to the House.

It didn't get any easier in the Senate. On the day we were heard in committee, the LHSAA was well represented; I recognized some of the principals. One of the lawmakers took her district out of the legislation by an amendment. I understood that she was against the legislation. She had a vote to express her opposition, but to remove her district from the effect of a law seemed a pretty extreme step to take, one that totally disregarded the homeschoolers in her district. She also admitted in committee that her reason for a particular vote was to support an amendment that was intended to give the bill trouble. She commented in committee that the legislation would be unfair because the homeschool athlete would have the advantage of a home cooked meal. Seriously, why not be grateful if they had a good meal? My children often have sandwiches, and I don't have the advantage of buying in bulk or from institutional wholesalers. I couldn't imagine complaining about that. Now that we are allowed to participate, I have volunteered to help cook some meals for the athletes, not for any "unfair" advantage, but because their coach is a bit of a health nut and wants to emphasize to his team that nutrition is important. I don't think the LHSAA has ever determined any food restrictions for the sake of "fair" competition. I was told by one senator on the committee that he could have stopped the bill in committee if he had wanted to. What did that mean? His comment made it seem so much more like a game or politics than an effort to make good law. We were so naïve at times to the way things worked. Yet knowing God knew everything, was in control, and was at work for our good, took away much of the frustration of dealing with the politics.

The committee had failed to deal adequately with the problem created by the "public/private amendment" which set us up for amendments on the Senate floor. There were very few votes that we were absolutely sure about, and unlike in the House, we had not spent as much time talking to the senators. The senators were not as accessible as the House Representatives. They had their own offices and often used corridors that didn't have public access.

We made it through the Senate Education Committee, but HB 531 had a rough road ahead on the Senate floor.

Chapter 9

Chaos, Confusion, and Flying Amendments

The window at the end of the corridor, where Jerrie said, "Pull the bill, Cameron."

Our experiences at the capitol were usually very positive. I was impressed by the heart and skill of many of our leaders. In the midst of a very political environment, many were very true to both their constituents and a sense of doing the right thing. Though their differences were very obvious at times, their camaraderie as a body seemed strong.

In some conflicts, chaos and confusion seem orchestrated to a certain end. When HB 531 went to the Senate floor in 2009, there was a lot of confusion; some of it seemed planned. The confusion started over an amendment that fixed the concerns brought up by the "public/private amendment." That was followed by what I called "flying amendments." Amendments came one after another; one took a district out of the bill while another put a part of that parish or district back in. Even more were posted on-line. There was a point when I didn't think everyone knew on what they were voting. In the midst of the confusion, a particular senator proposed an amendment which created the crime of falsifying grades to gain athletic eligibility; no one objected. We didn't even know what the amendment said before it was already adopted. Everything happened so fast. Because I'll refer to it later, and don't want to identify it by the senator who proposed it, I'll call this amendment the "penalty amendment." I was horrified that this was how law was being made. It was as if the wisdom of the process was being ignored, and politicians were using strategy to stop what they didn't have the votes to prevent. There was more going on here than met the eye, and I knew no one was going to really explain to us what had happened. I had a sick feeling in my stomach, and I joined Hozana on the balcony. I was struggling with my own composure, and didn't want to add to the discouragement Hozana probably felt as he watched all this. He said to me, "Mom, why are they so against us?" I didn't think I could go much longer without crying, so I told Hozana I had to go to the restroom. I cried, splashed some water on my face, and asked God for strength. I called Jerrie asking her to pray for me and returned to find Hozana. I told Liz I'd call her later; I didn't want to talk to anyone. I just wanted to leave. As awful as I felt, I knew God was sovereign and that I could trust Him. This was difficult, but it got worse.

HB 531 headed back to the House where Cameron asked the representatives to NOT concur with the Senate amendments. Then it was sent to a Conference Committee to resolve the differences between the House and the Senate.

A Conference Committee sounds like a meeting of some kind, but here's how it works: The President of the Senate and the Speaker of the House each appoint three members to the committee, one of those three being the lawmaker that carried the legislation on that side. Of the six, two from each side must sign the agreed upon language, which would usually be some kind of compromise on the differences. All six did not necessarily have to discuss the details, but at least four must agree with the final details. It was easier for me to understand when I saw a few groups of lawmakers huddled together obviously trying to hash out differences in the language of a bill. I also saw lobbyists quite involved in this process, and realized that politics played a large role, much of the negotiating being done behind the scenes. Obviously, the Speaker of the House and the President of the Senate played a huge roll in all this, being able to choose the conferees.

Most of the differences between the language of HB 531 coming from the House and Senate were easy to agree upon. The conferees knew the wording needed to be changed back to the original concerning the "public/private amendment." They also knew that taking out districts wouldn't work in the bill. The main point of contention was the "penalty amendment" which created the crime of falsifying grades to gain athletic eligibility. It went so far as to strip a homeschooler of their state approval, which had implications for the funding of and access to a college education.

We were baffled that this was even an issue since the bill already narrowed the application of the law to homeschoolers who'd been approved by BESE, approval which already required verification of the adequacy of their education. As well, the current required GPA for athletes was a 1.5, which was "below average." Had this "penalty amendment" been suggested in committee, we would have had an opportunity to discuss the facts. I doubt a majority of the senators would have voted for such an amendment, but since this amendment was slipped in without discussion, it was not challenged.

Our concern with the amendment was the language that gave homeschoolers no protection from unwarranted accusations and investigations. As well, the penalties to other student athletes and their families were not nearly as severe. There were already established penalties for athletes and schools that falsified grades or other documents to gain eligibility. Why should homeschool athletes be treated any differently?

There was no difficulty with the conferees from the House, but to this day, I don't know exactly what transpired with the Senate conferees. Everything revolved around the "penalty amendment" added by a particular lawmaker on the Senate floor. He insisted he was only trying to help, but his amendment was a source of great trouble. The Senate President told me that he appointed favorable conferees for us. To the contrary, he appointed conferees that had both expressed strong opposition to the bill.

For most of the day we waited. We suggested that a notarized statement of the grades be required. They didn't go for that, and instead suggested a penalty of a $500 fine and a six month prison sentence. After seeking the advice of an attorney, we suggested additional language that would give homeschoolers protection against unwarranted accusations and investigations. They didn't go for that either. They suggested different combinations of the $500 fine, the six month prison sentence, and giving up approval from the state. Who is "they"? I'm not real sure. There were various parties and agendas at work behind the scenes; we were not privy to those conversations. As well, a certain amount of "he said" or "they said" gave anonymity to the sources of suggestions which would be unpopular. After all, who wants to be associated with putting homeschool moms in jail over a disagreement about grades? Who was really pulling the strings behind the scenes? I didn't know.

Knowing who was really for or against the legislation was at times quite difficult. Lawmakers were not always transparent about their agendas or participation in the process. Some politicians are very good at making things seem to be what they are not. Those against us could make themselves seem to be for us. They could also make those who were for us, appear to be against us. It is cowards who hide behind their schemes. They didn't realize that God and many others knew what they were doing.

It's easy to forget a lot of the details, but there were some moments that felt like a scene in a Norman Rockwell painting, the details frozen in my mind. One such moment was a conversation on the last day of the session dealing with the "penalty amendment."

Upon entering the front of the capitol building, you find yourself in Memorial Hall which is 2 stories high and about 120 feet long. It's huge. To the left is the Senate Chamber, and to the right is the House Chamber. In the middle, on the floor between the entrance and the main elevators is a large, bronze relief map of Louisiana encircled by the names of her 64 Parishes. On many days during the session, the hall is filled with student groups, tourists, and the echo of their conversations. Often, along the walls beside the statues of Governors, there are exhibits by various organizations. They are usually distributing literature, but often give out refreshments trying to draw attention to their causes. On the first day of the session and when high profile legislation is being debated, the media may be doing interviews in the hall. On the last days of the session law makers walk back and forth following legislation on both sides.

About 10 feet on the Senate side of the bronze floor map, someone was trying to explain to me that they had to include some kind of penalty in the language of the legislation. "Negative emotion" would be a good description of his countenance. With his eyes wide open and his brow lowered, he bent forward and wagged his finger in my face as he said, "Ms. Arceri, there must be a penalty!" I stepped backward since he was a bit in my space. He stepped forward again. Emphasizing each word, he said, "You don't understand. There must be a penalty!" I had little to say; I stepped back again. It was a bit crazy that last day. It was as if people just wanted to pass legislation, regardless of what was required to do so. Did they think we'd give up our rights to play baseball? Fortunately for us, Cameron was prepared to allow our input on changes. Anything can happen to legislation in a conference committee; we needed the legislation to be written right, or we planned to have it pulled.

Another one of those moments frozen in my mind like a photo was from that same last day of the session. In a hallway off the back of the Senate Chamber, there's a corridor that goes between the two chambers where the President of the Senate and the Speaker of the House have offices. At each end of the hall there's a window with a marble sill big enough for someone to sit. It was in front of that window that our attempts that second year ended.

I can still picture Representative Henry going over some scribbled notes with us, the paper resting on the sill. He had been going between us and significant senators, trying to agree on language to go through the conference committee.

Finally, the offer came that shut down the negotiations. They wanted us to give up our right to homeschool if they could prove our grades were wrong. This was not like any negotiating I'd done before. You know how when you haggle over a price, each offer gets closer to center of the two? Well, in this case each offer got worse, the last being so absurd that it was easy to just say, "no." (Perhaps that was the intention all along.) We stood shocked by the proposal. Jerrie was the first to speak. She said, "Pull the bill, Cameron." It was over for now.

We gathered in the hall with a few homeschoolers and friends. As we huddled together to pray, I couldn't hold back the tears that fell silently on my cheeks. I was disappointed for my sons, and knew we would face difficult decisions before the end of the summer. The ride home was especially hard for me. We were all tired, and each of us was dealing with the disappointments of the day. They say you try to block out bad memories – I don't remember the rest of that day too well. We were all exhausted.

It was quite disheartening to pull the bill the last day, but we had decided before we ever started that we would not do what we believed was unfair to homeschool athletes, or homeschool families in general. It was disheartening, but it wasn't difficult to make the right choice. We saw a lot of deals being made in the capitol. On this issue we didn't want a deal; we wanted what was fair.

There's a verse in the Bible that says, "I had fainted unless I had believed to see the goodness of the Lord…" I have been through times in life that showed me believing for God's best is a good guard against despair. Sometimes, even when things in the end don't go as you'd like, to expect and hope for God's goodness makes the going so much better. Expectation and hope lead to faith which is a far surer place to be. I'd rather have the assurance of things hoped for, but hope and expectation themselves guard against despair and faintness of heart. It was as if, in the midst of what could be so disappointing, God's grace placed me where I couldn't place myself, a place of trust.

I didn't really have much time to be disappointed. The LHSAA claimed they would take care of this problem themselves without legislation. I didn't think that would happen, but their claims might open a door for the upcoming school year. Things weren't looking good, but I clung to God's promise that I could trust Him.

Chapter 10

Relief

God knew our family needed some encouragement. Chris was ready for us to enroll Hozana in school again. Hozana was really bummed. I hated to see my sons discouraged, and I continued to remind them that God had a plan. I told them this would all work out well, somehow. At this point my words were very much words spoken by faith. I could see no solution on the horizon. Chris was ready for us to enrolled Hozana in school, but he gave me through the end of the summer to find a school in our district that would be willing to take the LHSAA up on the claims they made in the legislature. My soul took a deep breath. I was sure that I could trust God, that He was sovereign, and that His will was good, acceptable, and perfect. I set out to meet with principals in our district.

The problem without legislation was that the LHSAA rules regarding homeschoolers were very ambiguous. The LHSAA Commissioner had explained that the word "enrolled" could be interpreted to mean "on a list in the office," and the word "transcript" could mean "a file in the office." It was awkward suggesting to principals that the rule in their LHSAA handbook didn't really mean what it appeared to say, and that the Commissioner would verify this if they called him asking the right questions.

I spoke to or met with most of the principals in our district. I tried to be very direct, giving them all the information I had, and assuring them I was okay with their just saying "no." It was much easier to deal with their simply turning down our request, than their giving us no particular answer. Principals had to go through a lot of other people before they could make a decision on a matter for which they probably had no policy in place. The idea might appeal to the principal but not the school's board, or it might appeal to the athletic department, but not the administration. I not only had to find a principal willing to go along with this strange interpretation, but I also had to find a school where the board, the athletic department, and the administration were all willing to allow our participation.

A friend called to tell Chris that a private school in our district had a new principal who may be open to helping us. It certainly wouldn't hurt to go see him. The new principal and the administration welcomed us with open arms. That principal was only at the school for one year. He was willing to enroll the boys and accept our transcripts even though the boys were not attending any classes. There were still some hurdles to overcome, but before the end of basketball season, the boys were eligible.

Having the boys eligible to play ball took some of the stress out of the situation and put a little wind in our sails to pursue the issue further.

Chapter 11

The Baseball Bird

Zephyr Field, where I filmed the baseball bird

In the fall of 2009, before we obtained eligibility at the private school in our district, Hozana and Israel were playing baseball at a local "off-season" training league. The coaches were excellent, the players were from local high schools, and the games were played in the nearby minor league stadium. One evening when almost everyone had gone, but before the lights went out, I noticed a bird flying round and round the field, never landing, but circling the infield and outfield. With my camcorder in hand, I started taping its flight wondering if it would land. The bird would glide so close to the ground in the infield, and then soar in a circle around the outfield. This went on for several minutes till it began to loop higher each round, and finally exited the stadium in the lights.

After the 2009 legislative session, I was getting tired, and running out of options. Something about that bird stuck with me. I like playing with video and music; it's a creative outlet for me, a therapeutic distraction in my busy schedule. I downloaded the film and put it to Phil Driscoll's "Wait on the Lord." As I watched the video I saw images in my mind of my boys playing ball, and daydreamed a bit about the legislation passing. I edited clips of the boys playing baseball into the video. Watching the video on my computer became a way for me to meditate on the idea of waiting on the Lord. The words of the song are from Isaiah 40:28-31:

Hast thou not known? Hast thou not heard that the everlasting God, the LORD, the Creator of the ends of the earth, fainteth not, neither is weary? There is no searching of his understanding. He giveth power to the faint; and to them that have no might he increaseth strength. Even the youths shall faint and be weary, and the young men shall utterly fall: But they that wait upon the LORD shall renew their strength; they shall mount up with wings as eagles; they shall run, and not be weary; and they shall walk, and not faint.

I used the video to encourage myself in the Lord. The boys would kid with me sometimes saying, "Mom, what are you doing with that? It's just a bird." To everyone else it was Mom's video of the baseball bird, but to me it was a reminder that God would increase my strength as I waited upon Him. It became a fun project as I added more clips of the boys every couple of weeks.

After the bill passed, when I opened the file and watched the video, I cried tears of joy realizing how faithful God had been to keep His promises. He is so good!

Chapter 12

HB 303 - The 2010 Session

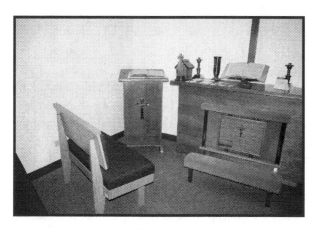

There's a Chapel in the capitol

During the 2009 legislative session, the LHSAA claimed that legislation was unnecessary because they would handle this on their own. Instead of handling the problem, in January they voted to make all homeschool athletes ineligible. Starting on July 1st, their new policy would read, "A student in a homeschool program shall be ineligible for interscholastic participation at a LHSAA member school." Well, it was clearer than their last policy.

Our boys were now playing at a private school, and unless the legislation passed in the upcoming session, Hozana would be ineligible his senior year as a homeschool athlete. We were aware of other student athletes who were in the same position as Hozana. One of those students was Avery Hall. She and her mom, Becky, helped us at the capitol. Becky had actually attended the LHSAA meeting where they voted on the new policy. It was very encouraging to meet other families who shared our concerns.

Chris and I felt as though Cameron had already given so much effort to this. We let him know that we felt he had represented us well, even if he carried it no further. I was encouraged by how quickly he expressed that he had no intention of quitting.

There was little attention on Prep sports in our area at the moment; the Saints had just won the Super bowl!

In February, Arlene and I got together with Cameron to talk about the upcoming session. We discussed what we could do to avoid the problems we had during the last session. To address the previous problems with the "penalty amendment," we added a section to the bill to clarify that homeschoolers would be subject to the same LHSAA penalties as other students. We also moved the section addressing participation in nonpublic schools forward in the bill to avoid the confusion initiated the previous year by the "public/private amendment." Otherwise, there was little difference from the previous bills; it was just a little clearer. We also added a few details to make the bill stronger, knowing some may try to water it down.

Arlene and I spent as much time as we could during the Mardi Gras holidays to organize our efforts. We had a productive meeting in Lafayette with other homeschoolers, and begin putting out updates by email.

Governor Jindal put the legislation on his education agenda which meant we'd have some extra help this time. This made a huge difference. We started the session with seventeen co-sponsors. It was very encouraging to see members of the Governor's staff working on the legislation. Arlene and I felt like the Calvary had arrived. Erin Bendily was the Education Policy Advisor for Governor Jindal's office, and assisted with the legislation.

One of the things we did differently in 2010 was an effort to communicate to the legislators that they had constituents who wanted them to support HB 303. We knew that it was hard for people to come to the capitol, which was where the lawmakers were during the session. We had people across the state send us signatures on a statement requesting the representative or senator's support. The tricky part was being sure all the signatures on each sheet were from the same Senate or House district. People listed their home address and phone number when they signed. Fortunately there are some smart homeschool parents out there who were able to figure out the districts from maps, and get the signed sheets to us before we went to committee. I still had some signature sheets arriving in the mail after we had compiled them for the Education Committee. In both the House and Senate Education Committees, we placed on each lawmaker's desk a stack of more than a hundred pages of signatures, the pages from their own district on top. We hoped this would counter the LHSAA's repeated statements that they had more than 250 member principals who did not want this legislation. Those principals didn't come to the Committee meetings, and many of them did not contact their representatives. I'm sure the lawmakers could see that our support was growing over time even with the public.

Our first hurdle of the 2010 session presented itself before the bill was even posted. There's a lobbying group in the capitol that represents Nonpublic, Private and Catholic school interests, particularly Educational Choice. They are a fairly large and well respected group. I believe there were opponents to the bill which tried unsuccessfully to draw this group into giving us trouble in 2009.

During the 2009 session, Israel was playing his last year in the parish league. Many of the other players attended some of the private schools in the area. After the bill was amended in the House, we began hearing from some of the parents of those players. They said they were receiving emails against our bill asking them to call their senators, the emails coming from their association with the schools. This happened very quickly without anyone even talking to us about their concerns. Fortunately, we were able to contact the lobbying group which was responsible for the emails, and show them the part of the bill which protected their discretion in the matter. At that point their attorney got involved and we allowed him to give us additional language to clarify the issue, language which we amended into the bill. I thank God that people told us about the emails. Knowing about those emails allowed us to stop what could have been a huge campaign against the legislation.

In the 2010 session we planned to avoid any misunderstanding by contacting the lobbyist right away, letting him know that we were using his attorney's language again to address their concerns. To our surprise, they wanted to make more amendments than satisfied them the prior year. Some of the changes they wanted to make were in sections of the bill that didn't apply to nonpublic schools. I thought some of the language they were suggesting would not accomplish what they were requesting; it was much more than what was needed. Though we trusted their intentions, and considered them friendly to our cause, we felt the amendments may eventually cause us problems. We planned to meet with their lobbyist and attorney to work things out.

This meeting was to take place at the capitol after the Governor addressed the legislature on the opening day of the session. Cameron and Erin were running late for the meeting because of the Governor's address, and we started the meeting assisted by a legislative analyst from the House Education Committee. Somehow we ended up in a stuffy room that had no air conditioning. I realized in the meeting that the attorney represented clients who may already be biased against the legislation. (I had seen their comments in an email that had been forwarded to me.) I felt a bit outnumbered when the legislative analyst appeared more interested in the lobbyist's concerns than ours. About that time I got a text from Cameron asking how it was going. My son Israel was with me. Because he is much quicker with texting, I handed him the phone asking him to text Cameron back that we needed help. It wasn't long before Cameron and Erin showed up. There was a much different tone when it wasn't just me in the room. Things were still unresolved, and Cameron was later asked to attend a meeting at Jesuit High School with some of the Catholic School Principals to address their concerns.

Cameron did a great job at that meeting. In response to so many of their questions he repeated that the legislation allowed them to just say no to homeschoolers if they didn't like the idea. He explained that the legislation would allow them to make the choice, and that they could make their own rules about that participation as long as they followed LHSAA policy. Before the meeting, I introduced myself to the principal of Ursuline Academy where I had attended high school; I hoped to find some common ground. After the meeting, I had a principal question me about why Cameron was helping homeschoolers. He said it seemed like he was just doing this because I was his constituent. I told him that I believed that had a lot to do with it, and that I thought it was a good thing that he represented the concerns of his constituents. Wasn't that the idea of a representative government?

Their suggestions concerned us, mostly because we didn't think all of them were necessary, but also because there may be unintended consequences. Cameron and Erin thought we needed to go along with their requests. In previous years when we were concerned, we were hesitant to be too bold with our opinions, trying to be realistic about our inexperience. However, we had learned the hard way that hesitancy had a down side at times. I was often in the position to pray for wisdom. I think one answer to those prayers was the sense that we had to balance trust with vigilance about detail. On this one it was obvious we had to trust Erin and Cameron. Before agreeing to the amendment, we asked for something in return.

We were aware of a set of talking points against our bill that were posted by the LHSAA on their website, even though they claimed they were neutral on the legislation. The talking points were written by someone associated with one of the schools that was a member of the lobby group that suggested these amendments. I suggested that we would allow the amendments if their members and clients would refrain from speaking against the bill. They agreed.

Before one of my visits to Baton Rouge, I thought I should check the BESE website to see if there was anything going on there about our bill. On the same day I was to visit the capitol, BESE was approving the Legislative Action Plan, and HB 303 was listed as "Support if amended." What did that mean? I sent a message to Cameron and Erin, and planned to stop by the Department of Education while I was there. A couple of people joined me at the capitol and went with me to the LDE. I was surprised how helpful the Department was, and I'm glad we stopped by since there had been an error on the report which would not have been good for us. They assured us that they were recommending that BESE support the legislation as it was. We followed through by attending the meeting to be sure it was changed.

God said He was sovereign, and I could trust Him. I saw His sovereignty very clearly when we looked back at what had happened to the bill in the House Education Committee. Sometimes things that appear to be problems and challenges turn out for good. I think of Joseph, the son of Jacob, the son of Isaac who was the son of Abraham. He had been sold into slavery by his brothers, but later in life he told them that what was meant for evil was turned for good. We all know the story of how he became a prince in Egypt able to save his family from famine. I believe a big part of God's sovereignty in our lives is His ability to cause all things to work together for our good, which is all the more reason to trust Him.

When we went to the House Education Committee this amendment opened a can of worms (*a complex, troublesome situation arising when a decision or action produces considerable subsequent problems*). Adding an entire page of language to a four page bill, language that would protect private schools, begged the public school advocates to ask, "What about us?" Though I knew it was inevitable that the language about lawsuits and unquestionable discretion given to the principals would be extended to the public schools, I found myself motivated to strongly object in the Committee meeting, even though I could sense Cameron was ready to concede. This was the fourth time I was sitting at one of those tables facing a panel of legislators. The first time, Arlene and I could sense cues from Cameron by the way he moved his hand on the table when we spoke. This time I didn't even need to look at Cameron or Erin. It seemed all the air around me was saying, "Don't say anything." I awkwardly spoke up, reading a part of the Louisiana Constitution regarding education and expressing that I didn't think this was fair. As the discussion continued, I could sense a lump in my throat, and my eyes wanting to water as I realized they wanted to give state employees and tax funded schools the discretion to discriminate against Louisiana students for reasons that could be totally prejudicial. As a woman who is usually quite composed, I'm not real familiar with methods of holding back tears, but I've seen how men swallow a lot in very emotional situations. So, I reached for the water pitcher on the table. I refilled a couple of times. I don't know if it was the water or the swallowing, but it took away that horrible "I think I'm going to cry" kind of feeling. I think one of the representatives could sense my frustration. He looked at me very kindly and talked about how we should have known the amendment would lead to this.

When the Bill went to the House floor there was more confusion as the attempt to amend the bill didn't thoroughly remove the language they were trying to amend. It looked as if we were trying to pull a fast one; we weren't. They had to take it off the floor briefly to address the issue. We didn't object to further amending since we knew what the intent of the committee had been.

Looking back, there were three good things that came from this struggle over the amendment:

First, it was hard for principals and the LHSAA to argue against something that was totally optional. According to the bill, they could just say, "no." We gave that discretion to the principals in the original version of the bill in 2008. This brought us back to our original, which was very similar to laws in other states. These amendments nearly guaranteed the bill would sail through the Senate.

Second, homeschool athletes would have to seek schools that wanted them rather than wrestle with schools that didn't. The legislation would allow them, by sitting out a year, to go out of district to find a private school that would allow their participation. This would be similar to the way a parent might look for a school they wanted their child to attend. It may take time, but many schools will become less resistant after time and experience with homeschool families.

Third, all the fuss and attention to this issue caused people to ignore other details in the bill. No one questioned the wording on districts which would allow homeschoolers the same district allowances as other athletes. Also ignored was the language to protect homeschoolers from principals determined to put homeschoolers through a barrage of academic tests to play ball. We made sure that for public schools the academic documents were limited to those specified in the bill, which were very adequate.

Lobbying the third year was easier than previous years. By now we were a little more organized, and at least knew most of the legislators by name. I think most of the lawmakers didn't know who we were or what particular bill we were advocating, but they recognized our faces as familiar, which made it easier for us to initiate conversations.

Realizing that many of the lawmakers would not know the legislation hadn't passed the previous year, Jerrie recommended we reintroduce ourselves as the session began, and explain to them what happened at the end of the previous session. Even though we were becoming more fluent in conversations with the lawmakers, props still helped. We made some promotional, flipping coins. It was easy to say, "Hi Senator. Did you get your flipping coin?" Most at least smiled when they looked at our "unofficial" legislative flipping coin with a "yea" on one side and a "nay" on the other. We gave them the coin in a small envelope that read, "Don't let your vote be the flip of a coin. Read the bill, Talk to the author, and do the right thing."

Chris went with me to Baton Rouge at the beginning of the session. It was my favorite day at the capitol having him there with me on a day that was not controversial. I could sense him watching me and smiling while I talked to lawmakers. We went out to lunch and had a wonderful day. I thank God that Chris was as supportive as he was throughout this three year ordeal. It took so much longer than I expected, and he didn't want to see me giving so much effort to something that looked as if it wouldn't succeed. Chris had been taking up some of the slack at home when I went with Arlene to the capitol. He can do a lot of his work from home which made it possible for me to go without the boys allowing them to get their studies done, and make it on time to baseball practice. I'm sure the boys didn't mind since Dad was more likely to order pizza for lunch and was more lenient with their chores.

We had a family meeting before the 2010 session, and everyone agreed to cooperate as much as possible at home with their studies, chores, and attitudes to make it easier to get through the distractions that might come during the session. When the bill passed, we went out to eat together to celebrate, and we were all glad it was finally over. More than once my children have expressed their appreciation. Though I was motivated by the needs of homeschool athletes across the state, my children were the inspiration for my efforts. Continuing to homeschool them while they play high school ball is my reward. I believe that in God's sovereignty He probably had more purposes in all this than we will ever know. It's just another chapter in our lives and the lives affected by God's work in us.

I cannot begin to write all the things that happened in these three years. There were so many times when God encouraged our hearts and directed us. So often Arlene and I felt God's leading to do things. Very often we'd receive information just when we needed it, or unexpectedly run into someone we needed to see. We had such fun talking about what God had done as we traveled to and from Baton Rouge. Once we were on the interstate we usually called Chris and Craig to give them a report of what had happened, and let them know we were headed home.

During the 2010 session, the chapel was my first stop when I went to the capitol. God led me to consider the armor of God spoken of in Ephesians. I asked Him to guard my mind and thoughts with His salvation, to guard my heart and emotions with His righteousness, to secure me in His truth, to help me use faith when confronted, and to use His Word to discern the motives of hearts around me. I asked Him to prepare me to walk unashamed of the gospel which can reconcile all men to Himself.

One day while praying in the chapel the Lord spoke to my heart. When I say the Lord spoke to my heart, I mean just that. The Bible says the sheep know the voice of their Shepherd. I became a Christian in 1979, my first year of college at LSU. There were many people who had a profound influence on my life as I began to walk with the Lord. One in particular was a young man named Bill, who was the first to help me understand the value of the Word of God and prayer.

At the time, Bill was teaching a Campus Crusade for Christ Leadership Training Class on campus. He said to me, "You can meet with the living God of the universe." He suggested using a Bible and a notebook. I didn't have a Bible at the time, but I borrowed one that night and couldn't wait to begin this dialogue with God the next morning. I was told that the Bible was God talking to me, and prayer was my talking back. How simple! With a very childlike faith, I wanted to read every Word God had written. It wasn't long before I had to reckon with the issue of the Bible being true, all of it. In my heart I knew it was true even if I didn't understand it. I'm a very analytical person about most things, but this was something I knew I needed to do by faith and from within. It wasn't an academic thing. It was beyond my limited intellect or natural abilities. I made the decision that I was going to believe the Bible is God's Word, and that God's Word is true. After that, God provided very adequate explanations for what would have previously seemed impossible or even contradictory to what I'd been taught or known. To this day, the Bible remains my absolute source of Truth. Truth has led me to a very personal relationship with Jesus who calls Himself the Truth. He is not silent like a man-made God or idol. He speaks to me in many ways, usually by His written Word and His Spirit within me. So, when I say the Lord spoke to my heart, I'm talking about Jesus, who loves me enough to talk to me.

Getting back to the capitol chapel, God said to me, "I have all authority in this place. There are people here who seem to have a lot of power and influence. Don't be intimidated. They have no power that I haven't given them, and I am in you."

He encouraged me by reminding me that He was with me. With that I felt much more confident to speak to lawmakers. At every turn, God was there, encouraging me, guiding me, correcting me. Some people had connections with Senator Chaisson, the President of the Senate. Some could walk right into the Governor's office. But I had connection with God, and access to His throne at any time I needed it. I knew that though I usually felt like a fish out of water,

God would provide whatever I needed for where He was leading me.

I wouldn't want it to appear that I was always aware of God's purposes, and seldom waivered in my confidence and trust. One of the things I look forward to in heaven is the absence of darkness, sin, doubts, fears and tears. Besides the obvious struggles I dealt with because of my circumstances, I think the most difficult were those moments of doubt when I questioned myself and what I was doing.

I remember one of those times during the third session when I was on the interstate headed to the capitol. Throughout the ride to Baton Rouge I had faced discouraging thoughts. "What if it doesn't pass? What if you're wasting your time? What if you are too stubborn to quit? What if you just don't want to face the truth and the reality that this won't work?" And then as I approached the exit I thought, "What if this isn't God's will and I'm on my own?" With that question, God interrupted my thoughts, and said, "Lisa, trust Me. I am with you, and will never leave you." Boy, did I need to hear that! I knew it, but God knew I needed to be reminded at that moment. I was continually exposed to people, strangers and friends alike, who did not agree with my decision to homeschool in high school or to pursue this legislation. There were a few times when I had one difficulty after another.

One of the more difficult experiences was when someone I expected to be for the legislation was against it. It's not uncommon for someone who has a certain cause to find resistance from the most unlikely places. I knew not everyone would understand, and I needed not to take it to heart. To pass legislation, your purpose must be established, your steps sure, and your direction straightforward or you'll quit. There are just too many obstacles for the faint of heart.

There were times when I knew some of my family's needs were being put aside to take care of this; that was especially hard. I knew it was probably even a good thing for the boys to do a little more work to help out at home, but I hated things being less organized. I had actually organized more just to manage my home and the boy's schoolwork while pursuing this, but that required making decisions about what was a priority. There wasn't as much time for the fun stuff which was difficult for everyone.

I asked my youngest son what was the hardest part for him about my being busy with all this. He said he didn't mind making his own sandwiches, but liked them better when I made them. He said the food wasn't as good when I was busy. My middle son said it was a bummer that his birthday was during the session. He also didn't like that we quit going swimming at Grandma's when the legislature was in session. My oldest said I was on the computer too much. They were right; we had to put some things aside to get the important things done. Fortunately, they said it was worth it. When the bill passed, my husband jokingly said he would finally have his wife back. As for me, as much as I hated the extra clutter and messes, I knew I could catch up on the housework. To the boy's dismay, after the bill passed we spent a week on yard work and maintenance around the house that had been neglected. The things I missed most were leisurely visits with friends and fewer distractions at home. There was a bit of a strain on my husband and I because of the uncertainty of things, but our love and patience with one another was much stronger than the stress. I believe our marriage was strengthened by our experience of support for one another through all this. I think he got a lot more flack than I did about us homeschooling the boys, and fighting this battle. I had a tremendous network of homeschool moms that supported me, but many of the people Chris saw day in and day out, including all those dads at the ball parks, didn't understand homeschooling. Fortunately, one of his best friends, a coach, was also a homeschool dad who even came to the capitol one day to help out.

We made it through the Senate Education Committee without amendments. If you look on line it will say it was reported without amendments on June 1st, but I know the day it went through the committee was May 27th because it was my 50th birthday. It was almost too easy.

In the Senate Education Committee, the President of the Louisiana Federation of Teachers spoke out against our legislation. He said that a school is a community, that we were not a member of that community and so should not enjoy the benefits of that community. He was concerned that passing this legislation would change the "fabric of that which we know as a school."

The Preamble of Article VIII of the Louisiana Constitution states:

> *The goal of the public educational system is to provide learning environments and experiences, at all stages of human development that are humane, just, and designed to promote excellence in order that every individual may be afforded an equal opportunity to develop to his full potential.*

Has the system itself and its individual campuses determined that they are themselves the community? Has their identity become bigger than the identity of the people who fund them? I'm sure he meant that the school is itself like a community, but by that definition there are implications of uniqueness distinct from the larger community they are within. It seems as though he wanted to define public schools as much more than an environment of learning, and that afforded equal opportunities to less than every individual. We should not forget that public schools are a service provided by the community, and to the community, but are not themselves independent of the community in which they exist. I believe at the core of most opposition to allowing our participation in sports was a matter of discrimination against a different form of education.

HB 303 was reported favorably.

As we left the Committee room there was an incident in the hallway with a very disgruntled opponent of the legislation, but Cameron stepped in to stop it. The Sergeant at Arms escorted our group out of the situation into one of those elevators usually reserved for the senators. The incident only involved someone raising their voice and getting in my face; I think they were just frustrated and didn't mean any harm. Nathan Aultman, a homeschool senior who had come to the meeting, stood next to me and said, "Ms. Lisa, I'll be your body guard." We all laughed and headed to the cafeteria to celebrate.

We didn't want to be overly confident, but we felt like we could finally see an end in sight. The next time we went to the capitol we had to regroup our original signature sheets by Senate districts to give to the senators. Arlene's children, Tanner and Riley, spent about an hour in the capitol cafeteria helping us sort and staple them into packets. Our last effort was to deliver these packets of signatures to some of the senators. It was probably the easiest thing we had done in the capitol. What senator wouldn't be open to someone delivering a signed message from their constituents? We had painstakingly checked each address to be sure the addresses were in their districts. Of all the things we gave to legislators, this meant the most to me because we were helping people communicate with the people that represented them.

About this same time, Louisiana was facing the crisis of the BP oil spill. Because of the attention needed to address issues related to the spill, the Senate began passing over controversial bills. Governor Jindal was also very busy addressing the oil spill. HB 303 was both controversial and on the Governor's agenda, so it had to wait. Finally, it was scheduled for debate.

Senator Walsworth carried the bill for us in the Senate. We were confident in his abilities, and knew he was committed to homeschoolers, but we were surprised that he didn't object to an unrelated amendment that was added to HB 303. When this amendment came up, we leaned over to see Erin's laptop. We asked, "What's that?" She didn't seem to know anything about it. When we read it we realized it had nothing to do with our bill. I personally feel like there should be rules against doing that. It defeats the purposes of the process that is in place to give people an opportunity to be represented in the making of laws.

The amendment did apply to the LHSAA; it just wasn't about homeschoolers. It wasn't even being added to the same section of law. Cameron told us he had talked to the LHSAA about the amendment. He said the LHSAA would not oppose the concurrence in the House. I pulled a legislative assistant aside and asked him if anyone had actually looked into this to make sure we weren't going to have further problems. I told him I was concerned for whoever this might affect. Who would it affect? He assured me that it would be ok; I didn't like it.

All we needed was a concurrence from the House, and I think it's rare for the members not to concur when the author asks for it. The bill was finally passed by a vote of 82 -13, but that vote did not reflect everyone who had supported us. One of the representatives that I had grown to respect as we worked through this process, and who had always supported us, did not vote for the concurrence because of the amendment that was slipped in. Though it would have made things difficult for us in the House since the Senate had adopted the amendment, it would be good if more legislators would reject these kinds of amendments. I respected his vote of "nay." It was like pork added to our bill, pork without a price tag. We're all aware of how this is done in Congress at our expense. I think Louisiana's better than that. The Legislature should restrain such methods in making law.

The day after the bill was concurred in the House, it was signed by the Speaker of the House and the President of the Senate. Then it went to the Governor to be signed, and became Act 691.

Governor Jindal signed the bill before the new LHSAA policy prohibiting homeschool participation went into effect. There is no doubt in my mind that his making our concerns a priority was instrumental in things working out as well as they did; God bless him.

As for us, our sons are playing ball at a private Christian school in our district, and we continue to homeschool. To my knowledge, 20 homeschool athletes were registered in 2010 to participate in LHSAA member schools. The LHSAA rewrote their homeschool policy, making it consistent with state law.

Chapter 13

More about the Choice to Homeschool

I had a principal ask me in a meeting why we were making sports so important that we'd go through all this. Some may be surprised to know that sports are not that important to me. We didn't do this because of sports. The issue of our son's access to sports was restricting our choice to continue homeschooling, which was important enough to go through all this. This story seems incomplete without some explanation of why homeschooling is so important to us.

In this discussion about why we choose to homeschool, I mean to make no implication about the choices other parents make. If there is any comparison it is only in the context of our decision for our own children. I think some of the objections to the legislation were really objections to why we homeschool. We often avoided the explanation because we felt it shouldn't be a part of the debate over participating in sports. However, an explanation for why we want to homeschool in high school may help some understand our persistence with the issue.

First of all, not everyone would want to homeschool in high school. Families homeschool for many different reasons. Some reasons are merely a matter of physical necessity or logistics, such as a family that lives in a place where schools are inaccessible, or a lifestyle that requires travel or schedules that cannot conform to a traditional school. Others homeschool for purely academic reasons. Perhaps their child is a prodigy or has exceptionalities that they are particularly prepared to address. Some homeschool because of a dissatisfaction with their experience of traditional schooling, but I think a larger number of homeschoolers do so to have more influence and involvement in their children's development.

We chose to homeschool before our children were old enough to go to school. I went to a meeting to get information about homeschooling when my oldest was still in a carrier. Shortly after Hozana was born, I hosted a "Young Moms" Bible study. We had very little furniture at the time, and we met in my front room which had a loveseat, a few folding chairs, and a pole lamp in the corner next to a goofy cushion chair that opened into a cot. I can still picture my friend Lisa sitting on that silly chair with a child on her lap saying, "Being a mom is a high calling from God." She explained that it was her destiny and profession at the moment, and that she wanted to use her gifts and abilities as she would in any other calling or profession. Her words inspired me; she gave such value to being a mom. At that time, we weren't thinking about high school or athletics; we were just trying to be dedicated moms.

I used to wear a shirt that read, "Every mom's a working mom." Many a mom commented to me about that shirt. At the time, even wanting to stay home with my young children was questioned, as if my choice to give up the financial advantages of a career was foolish. Would someone else replace my role with my children? It's not that I thought I was so capable. (Being a mother can be very humbling.) I just knew in my heart that it was my responsibility and pleasure.

When the boys were of school age, most people around me assumed the boys would begin kindergarten. I knew that much more than the alphabet and numbers would be taught to my children in classroom settings. They would be learning social habits from other children, some not so favorable. I saw my sons at that age like wet cement, being marked on and molded. Who would make those impressions on their hearts? I could just imagine the neurons and connections being made in their minds. Who would be training that young mind throughout the day?

As they got older, who would teach them the ways of the Lord? Could that be done on the side like an extracurricular activity? If I worked all day while my sons were with other people, would there be enough time between dinner and homework to share our lives with them? Would I be too tired to really pay attention? How were we supposed to give them wisdom if we weren't even privy to what they dealt with on a daily basis?

Our reasons for homeschooling have probably changed over time. Most homeschool families I know discover benefits they never considered. It wasn't until we had homeschooled for several years that we realized what an opportunity it was for the boys to strengthen their relationships as brothers. The time we are able to spend together as a family is priceless. Time goes by so quickly. It won't be long before, if Jesus doesn't come back first, our sons will be pursuing their purposes and dreams in life, and starting their own families. Teaching one-on-one has been efficient, allowing more time for areas that required more effort as well as more time to explore other interests.

Many families homeschool to provide a certain environment for their children's development. Personally, that was very important to us, but we were also concerned about the worldview that would be promoted through the curriculum, textbooks, literature and content of our children's lessons. I not only believe that God created the heavens and the earth in six days, but I also want my sons to see their studies of Life Sciences in the context of discovering what God has created. I want them to understand history in the context of what God was and is doing in the earth to accomplish His purposes. I want them to understand Geography and Earth Sciences knowing the events of creation and Noah's flood, which were instrumental in the initial formation of the landscapes they observe. I want them to understand the influence of paganism, Judaism and Christianity on the development of world politics and culture in the course of human events. I want my sons to read literature that is worth dwelling on, which would edify, encourage, and challenge them. I want them to understand the blessings of liberty we enjoy in America, and have an understanding of the United States Constitution and our rich Christian heritage. I want their study of physical sciences to be with the purpose to solve problems that benefit others, and their study of the arts to glorify God, not themselves. I could go on and on describing how I want through their education to emphasize that God is. I didn't want their knowledge to be without God. Our goals in education may be different than those in many schools.

I am amazed at how natural it is to teach lessons of character while homeschooling. Besides the opportunity to choose reading materials that teach valuable lessons, we have adequate time to admonish, encourage, and lead our children on a path that exposes them to the Truth of God's word in a practical way.

It wasn't an initial reason we chose to homeschool, but one of the greatest reasons we continue to homeschool is the opportunity to spend more time together as a family. I know we will never regret having made the choice to spend this time with our sons.

As the boys approached the high school years, some thought this was a time to stop homeschooling for reasons concerning "socialization." Though some argue "socialization" is a reason NOT to homeschool in high school, I would argue it is a strong reason FOR homeschooling in high school. High School is a time when young men and women are exploring ideas about how they identify themselves. While most agree they should be going towards a lifestyle of responsibility and independence, our culture can instead entertain and distract them, enabling them to have lifestyles focused on temporary gratification and consumption. They are making decisions that will have lifelong affects, choices regarding education, relationships, their response to authority, and how they will influence and be influenced by others. They are curious about what they will do with their lives. They are discovering their interests, talents, skills, and abilities. They seek affirmation, acceptance, purpose, value and meaning in life. None of these characteristics are unique to this age group alone, but due to the acceleration of their physical, emotional and cognitive development it appears to them and to others as a major initiation into the adult world.

If the idea of socialization is a matter of social opportunities, most now know that homeschoolers generally have plenty of opportunities to socialize with peers as well as a variety of age groups and types of people. The topic of socialization is covered in Louisiana's Civics textbooks. Having read one recently, I was surprised that the explanation of socialization in the textbook seemed to emphasize the importance of following the social rules or codes of the people around us, specifically our peers, rather than emphasize the importance of learning and valuing the rules and norms that are proven to work well for society. Is it possible that the socialization in some high schools is socialization that only works in high school, and might need to be unlearned after high school? If socialization is learning to adapt to cultural norms and ideologies, then it is of utmost importance to carefully select the groups to which our children would adapt, and the character of those from whom they would learn these ideologies. Socialization involves learning what behavior is acceptable when relating to others, and plays a part in the development of one's identity and personality. The very rules and norms learned in the socialization process may encourage young people to conceal the reality they live in, believing the norm that certain things should not be told to parents, which would allow students a certain freedom from or lack of access to the oversight or wisdom of their parents.

The experience in many (not all) of today's high schools is about so much more than academics. Many of today's schools are social sites. Though many would like to deny it, when speaking of socialization in many high schools, the reality is that we are not talking about knowing how not to stare at people or how to feel at ease with people from a variety of backgrounds. Though not the intent or goals of the system, we are talking about young people adapting to profanity and disrespect. We are talking about young people learning not to tell parents what goes on around them. We're talking about bullying, experimenting with drinking, drugs, sex and alternative life styles. We're talking about conversations about things that are perverted. We're talking about adapting to entertainment that is violent and sexually explicit. We're talking about learning to dress promiscuously, and learn patterns of speech and slang that won't work past high school. We're talking about adapting to a culture obsessed with romantic or sexual relationships for fun, defrauding each other. We're talking about communications that may corrupt good moral behavior. And that's not to mention the ideologies that may be promoted.

I do realize there are schools that do not allow their campuses to be an environment that supports a lack of character. I also recognize that there are strong families and teenagers who can weather even the worst of environments. However, it is undeniable that the social environment in most high schools has a negative effect on the character of many students.

So what about sports? Isn't the socialization of students on a team just as significant as attending school? Circumstances differ for each student. Many schools, even if only participating in their athletic program, may provide some very negative influences to a young person. Parents should carefully consider the circumstances and the strength of their son's or daughter's character before making this decision. Though athletic teams have a strong camaraderie, and as a team should have a great sense of identity and unity, the degree of socialization by the experience can be more easily managed as a homeschool athlete for at least three reasons: focus, supervision, and time.

The time spent on most good athletic teams is primarily spent focused on the sport itself in a rather structured environment. Athletes build trust in one another on the field and in play. Anyone who has played high school football knows the bond between players who face such a physically intense challenge together. However, the percent of time students spend with teammates that is not focused on sports is a choice of the particular athlete, and is often much less than the percent of time students on campus spend not focused on academics. What about weight rooms and locker rooms? No doubt there will be inappropriate conversations and behavior there because of a lack of supervision and accountability, but a mature homeschooler's frequent access and accountability to parents can address this.

Another difference is supervision. I remember the first day Hozana went to a traditional school. He came home and said, "Mom, kids curse more in school than they do in the dugout at the park!"

This surprised me, but one of the moms whose children had always gone to school said, "Well of course, Lisa. Parents and adults are usually in earshot of the dugouts at the park, so they keep it down." Even if not the best supervision, most aspects of sports are supervised or observed.

Finally, another reason a homeschool athlete's experience regarding socialization is different is because of time. It is still not "all day, every week day." In our experience, the time spent at home during the day homeschooling is still adequate enough to maintain the influence and involvement a parent needs to discuss issues and share wisdom.

When our children were as young as 10 years old, we had to teach them effective ways to deal with profanity in sports so they wouldn't begin using the same language. We were able to advise them on issues of discretion when avoiding a bad influence. As they got older, the issues changed and so did the advice, but the intent was the same, to avoid adopting the norms that were in conflict with our values and beliefs, and to be a blessing to others.

My son was in a traditional high school for a year. When Hozana was in school we usually stopped at his favorite coffee shop or snack spot on the way home to stay in touch. Though helpful, this would not have been very practical with multiple children in school, and may not have been effective after a period of time. Maneuvering successfully through today's teenage culture requires coaching, preferably from parents, who have time and access to their children's schedules, and who are able to maintain consistent and meaningful conversations with them.

It's a good thing to be socialized in the context of a loving family and community of friends and relatives where the norms have been tested over time. This may even reinforce a sense of identity that is not as constantly changing as the ideas of peers that are still relatively inexperienced with life.

On many high school campuses one of the difficulties for a student who has values contrary to the majority is the continuously negative input on those values, to a degree that would not be tolerated in the workplace and many other adult environments. To make things worse, most teenagers are more sensitive to social acceptance, making them more vulnerable to the pressure to conform to ideas and behavior they initially want to avoid.

As Christians we are instructed not to be conformed to the world, but to be transformed by the renewing of our mind. It is the truth of the Word of God that renews our mind and sets us apart from the world. It's challenging for us as parents to walk this out on a daily basis concerning the influences around our children. Jesus prayed for us that we would be kept from the evil in the world, and instructed us to pray that we would be delivered from evil. Our commitment and vigilance to lead our children in the ways of the Lord will not be popular, but it is an inalienable right given to us by God, and historically recognized in the United States. This goes against some concepts of socialization, and some norms of our culture, which is why I think this issue of socialization is so contentious.

The devaluing of the American family has created neediness in our youth for surrogates whom they find among peers and institutions other than the family. This is one of the characteristics of our society and culture that must be understood in order to prevent our children from embracing the ideas that would redefine the strong foundations of our society. The further we get from the ideal of strong family units, the harder it becomes to repair and restore what is being lost in our culture because our values are not reinforced to our youth.

I don't blame educational systems for the state of families in America, and I don't claim homeschooling to be a solution; it is a complex issue. I'm grateful for advocacy groups that make families a priority when considering law and policy. I applaud the Louisiana Department of Education for supporting this legislation which supported parental choice in education for many Louisiana families. In the Senate Education Committee the LFT President referred to the "fabric of that which we know as a school." I am more concerned about the fabric of that which we know as a family.

For us Homeschooling is about educating our children in a way that preserves the values and ideas we hold dear. May God bless everyone who has had even the smallest part in assisting us.

Chapter 14

The New Law

This chapter includes the actual language of the new Louisiana law that allows homeschool participation in Louisiana High schools. As with most laws, this is not the easiest read, and this chapter is more technical than the rest of this book. However, the law itself and its details are a very important part of this story. The language is very specific to prevent abuse, protect everyone's interests, and provide participation that is fair and reasonable to all involved.

Similar laws are written in other states. The language of such laws is unique to each state because of the differences in their homeschool laws, and the differences in the organization and policies of their athletic associations. Significant examples of this in Louisiana's new law are the exclusion to home study programs "approved" by the Board, and the specific conditions listed in Part B of the law. Details of process like the "written request for participation" and specific time frames were written for applicability. Many of the details may not have been necessary except to assure parties involved that there were no loop holes in the law for misuse.

Louisiana recognizes the rights of parents to educate their children at home. Louisiana does not require, but does allow both private schools and homeschools to seek approval of their programs from the Department of Education by verifying their adequacy. There are some advantages to obtaining the approval of the state such as recognition of diplomas, certain funding for college, and access to certain programs, but Louisiana rightly gives parents the choice about seeking that approval. Homeschool families that do not seek that approval must by law still register with the state to comply with current attendance and truancy laws.

No laws should be written that restrict a parent's liberty to teach their own children or make their own choices about their children's education. This new Louisiana law does not regulate homeschooling or the private schools which may choose to allow their participation. It only acknowledges the eligibility of certain homeschool athletes within certain guidelines providing a framework for the athletic participation of home study students in Louisiana high schools.

Research has shown that more regulation of homeschooling does not provide any better results on standardized test scores, but for purposes such as this participation in athletic competition, the same requirements already used for other acknowledgements seemed an appropriate standard to address the adequacy of the athletes' education. As well, requiring that athletes are in an approved home study program would prevent abuse of the law to get around academic eligibility issues. For those familiar with homeschool law in Louisiana, this is nothing new. Being in an approved home study program has been an option for homeschool students since 1984. Currently, this approval is prerequisite to accessing certain college funding and recognition of a homeschool diploma by state agencies and institutions. Had there been no academic requirements for non-homeschool athletes, this would not have been an issue as one of our goals was fairness. Because there were academic requirements for other athletes, it was a necessity. Using an already established standard just made sense.

Following is the body of the new law concerning homeschool athletes. Section A is introductory, and clarifies participation in public and nonpublic schools. The language in part (2) of A assures the discretion of the non-public schools, and clarifies that this law in no way regulates those non-public schools. Section B includes 7 conditions of participation. Section C includes specifics that prevent homeschooling from being used as a means of eligibility for students who would be otherwise ineligible. Section D acknowledges that homeschool athletes would be subject to the same athletic association penalties as other student athletes.

R.S. 17:236.3

R.S. 17:236.3. Home study program participants; eligibility to participate in interscholastic athletics; guidelines; standards; limitations.

A. Beginning with the 2010-2011 school year and continuing thereafter, a student in a home study program approved by the State Board of Elementary and Secondary Education in accordance with R.S. 17:236.1 shall be eligible as follows to participate in interscholastic athletic activities at a high school that is a member of the Louisiana High School Athletic Association:

(1) If seeking to participate at a public high school that is a member of the association, participation shall be in accordance with the provisions of this Section.

(2) (a) If seeking to participate at a state-approved nonpublic high school that is a member of the association, participation shall be at the sole discretion of the govern authority of the nonpublic school. If participation is permitted, the governing authority shall determine the terms and conditions of any such participation at the school. However, the student's participation shall be subject to the same requirements, policies, and rules of eligibility of the Louisiana High School Athletic Association as applicable to other students participating in the activity at that school, excluding any association requirements, policies, or rules that prohibit or restrict such participation by a student in a state-approved home study program.

(b) No person, individually or on behalf of any other person, shall have a cause of action arising from a denial of participation of a home study student in interscholastic athletics at a state-approved nonpublic high school or, if a home study student is allowed to participate under terms and conditions determined by the governing authority of the nonpublic school, from any refusal or denial by the nonpublic school of further participation by the student in interscholastic athletics at the nonpublic school.

(c) Nothing in this Subsection shall be construed as regulation of a private secondary school inconsistent with Article VIII, Section 4, of the Constitution of Louisiana.

B. To be eligible to participate in interscholastic athletics as provided by Subsection A of this Section, the home study student shall meet each of the following conditions and comply with other applicable provisions of this Section:

(1) The student shall be subject to the same residency or attendance zone requirements as other students participating in the athletic activity.

(2)(a) The student's participation shall be approved by the principal of the school providing the athletic activity.

(b) The student's parent or legal guardian shall make a written request for the student to participate in interscholastic athletic activities to the principal of the school providing the activity. Such requests shall be made not later than the first eleven days of the school year.

(c) The principal of the school providing the athletic activity shall approve or disapprove such written request within thirty days after receipt by the principal of all information and documentation requested by the principal from the student or the student's parent or legal guardian, or both. A request for information and documentation by the principal shall be limited to information and documentation that is required by this Section and information and documentation that is required of other students relative to participation in the athletic activity.

(d) A decision by the principal to approve or disapprove the written request for the student to participate shall be final.

(e) No person, individually or on behalf of any other person, shall have a cause of action arising from a denial by a public school principal of participation by a home study student in interscholastic athletics at the school or, if a home study student is allowed by the principal to participate under the terms and conditions provided by this Section from any refusal or denial of further participation by the student in interscholastic athletics at the school.

(3) After a decision is made by the principal to approve a request for the student to participate, the student then shall participate in any

tryouts for such activity at the same time and in the same manner as other students who want to participate in the same activity.

(4) At the time of participation in the athletic activity, the student and the student's home study program shall be in full compliance with all guidelines, standards, and requirements established by R.S. 17:236.1 for a home study program to be approved by the state.

(5)(a) The student shall meet academic standards required of other students to participate in the athletic activity.

(b) The student shall submit documentation from the State Board of Elementary and Secondary Education that the student is in a home study program approved by the board.

(c) The student shall submit a copy of his transcript showing units of study completed or in progress, the grades earned for such study, and his cumulative grade point average.

(6) The student shall meet all other standards and requirements applicable to a student participating in the athletic activity, including but not limited to tryouts, practice time, codes of conduct and student discipline, physical exams, proof of age, permission forms, waivers, required paperwork, fees, and transportation arrangements but excluding any requirements that the student be enrolled in or attend the school, or both.

(7) The student shall meet conditions applicable to students at the school relative to having any required insurance coverage either by participating, if otherwise eligible, in insurance programs offered through the school or school system or by providing for such insurance coverage in another manner.

C.(1) A student who has been enrolled in a public or nonpublic school during the school year in which the student begins home study or during the previous school year and who was determined ineligible to participate in one or more interscholastic extracurricular activities at such school for reasons related to student conduct or academic performance, or both, shall be ineligible to participate in interscholastic athletic activities as provided by this Section for one calendar year from the date the student was determined ineligible.

(2) A student who has been enrolled in a public or nonpublic school during the school year in which the student begins home study shall not be eligible to participate in interscholastic athletic activities as provided by this Section during the remainder of that school year nor during the following school year.

D.(1) Any home study student who provides or on whose behalf others provide any false representation, documentation, or verification of the student's qualifications for the purpose of meeting eligibility requirements to participate in interscholastic athletics shall be ruled ineligible to participate in accordance with policies of the Louisiana High School Athletic Association and shall be subject to the same penalties as other students as provided by the association.

(2) A school determined to be knowledgeable of any false representation, documentation, or verification of a home study student's qualifications for the purpose of meeting eligibility requirements to participate in interscholastic athletics shall be subject to penalties as established by the Louisiana High School Athletic Association for use of an ineligible student athlete.

Chapter 15

The Legislative Process

Following the legislative process requires getting the right information. We were fortunate to have been introduced to someone like Jerrie LeDoux who answered so many of our questions, and literally walked us through the process. We called her day and night. We asked a lot of questions and found clerks and support personnel to be tremendous sources of information. The legislative process in most states is available on-line, but the political process behind the scenes is learned by experience. We tried whenever possible to learn from the experience of others. We were told that lobbying was more about building relationships than persuasion. That was very good advice.

Louisiana laws are made by legislators from across the state. There are about 105 districts represented in the House, and about 37 districts represented in the Senate. Legislation can be initiated in either the Senate or the House, depending on the Senator or House Representative who authors the piece of legislation, called a bill. When filed, it is given a number. For example, a bill sponsored by one of the senators might be SB 735 (Senate Bill 735), whereas a bill sponsored by one of the House members might be HB 303 (House Bill 303).

There are specific rules that govern the process of a bill becoming law. It must receive a favorable vote to go through each step in order to proceed to the next. The bill must be read a certain number of times, be heard in certain committees, and eventually be supported by both the House and the Senate before it proceeds to the Governor to be signed into law.

This legislation was debated by and reported favorably by the House Education Committee before it was debated by the Full House. When it passed through the House, it was sent to the Senate, where it was referred to the Senate Education Committee for approval, before it was debated by the full Senate. In each step of the process, the language of the bill could be amended. In the end, the same language needed the approval of both the Senate and the House.

There are special rules and exceptions for certain circumstances, but this is generally how laws are made. Below is the History of the bills and resolutions (HB 871, HR 110, HB 531, and HB 303) that represent efforts to pass this legislation. Dates are listed starting from the most recent activity. As you will notice, the process takes time. This history only records the bill's progress as it successfully passed from one step to another. It does not show the many steps taken to prepare or work through the process. Nor does it list the 23 amendments which were adopted, withdrawn or rejected throughout the process. As I said at the beginning of Chapter One, many other stories could be told regarding this legislation. God was at work through these same events, in many more lives than our own. His sovereignty is often beyond our comprehension!

The following information is available on-line at *www.legis.state.la.us*:

HB 303 – 2010 Regular Session (Act 691)

06/29/2010 - Effective date: June 29, 2010.

06/29/2010 - Signed by the Governor. Becomes Act No. 691.

06/18/2010 – Sent to the Governor for executive approval.

06/17/2010 – Signed by the President of the Senate.

06/17/2010 – Enrolled and signed by the Speaker of the House.

06/16/2010 – Read by title, roll called, yeas 82, nays 13, Senate amendments concurred in.

06/15/2010 – Scheduled for floor debate on 6/16/2010.

06/14/2010 – Received from the Senate with amendments.

06/14/2010 – Rules suspended. Senate floor amendments were read and adopted. The amended bill was read by title, finally passed by a vote of 22 yeas and 10 nays, and ordered returned to the House. Motion to reconsider tabled.

06/03/2010 – Reported without Legislative Bureau amendments. Read by title and passed to third reading and final passage.

06/02/2010 – Read by title and referred to the Legislative Bureau.

06/01/2010 – Reported favorably.

04/22/2010 – Received in the Senate. Rules suspended. Read first and second time by title and referred to the Committee on Education.

04/21/2010 – Read third time by title, amended, roll called on final passage, yeas 70, nays 13. Finally passed, title adopted, ordered to the Senate.

04/21/2010 – Called from the calendar.

04/21/2010 – Read by title, amended, and returned to the calendar.

04/15/2010 – Scheduled for floor debate on April 21, 2010.

04/15/2010 – Read by title, amended, ordered engrossed, passed to 3rd reading – regular calendar.

04/14/2010 – Reported with amendments (12-2) (Regular).

03/29/2010 – Read by title, under the rules, referred to the Committee on Education.

03/12/2010 – First appeared in the Interim Calendar on 3/12/2010.

03/11/2010 – Under the rules, provisionally referred to the Committee on Education.

03/11/2010 – Pre-filed.

HB 531 – 2009 Regular Session

06/24/2009 – Notice House conferees appointed.

06/24/2009 – House conferees appointed: Henry, Austin Badon, and Hoffman.

06/23/2009 – Notice of Senate conferees appointed.

06/23/2009 – Senate conference committee appointed: Nevers, Donahue, and Morrish.

06/23/2009 – Notice House rejected Senate amendments.

06/23/2009 – Read by title, roll called, yeas 72, nays 18, Senate amendments rejected, conference committee appointment pending.

06/18/2009 – Scheduled for concurrence on 6/23/2009.

06/18/2009 – Received from the Senate with amendments.

06/18/2009 – Senate floor amendments read and adopted. The amended bill was read by title and finally passed by a vote of 22 yeas and 15 nays. The bill was ordered returned to the House. Motion to reconsider tabled.

06/17/2009 – Reported without Legislative Bureau amendments, read by title and passed to a third reading.

06/16/2009 – Committee amendments read and adopted. Read by title and referred to the Legislative Bureau.

06/15/2009 – Reported with amendments.

06/04/2009 – Received in the Senate. Rules suspended. Read first and second time by title and referred to the Committee on Education.

06/03/2009 – Read third time by title, amended, roll called on final passage, yeas 65, nays 35. Finally passed, title adopted, ordered to the Senate.

05/29/2009 – Scheduled for floor debate on 6/3/2009.

05/28/2009 – Read by title, amended, ordered engrossed, passed to 3rd reading – regular calendar.

05/27/2009 – Reported with amendments (7-6) (Regular).

04/27/2009 – Read by title, under the rules, referred to the Committee on Education.

04/18/2009 – First appeared in the Interim Calendar on 4/17/2009.

04/15/2009 – Under the rules, provisionally referred to the Committee on Education.

04/15/2009 – Pre filed.

HR 110 – 2008 Regular Session

06/16/2008 – Enrolled, signed by the Speaker of the House and taken by the Clerk of the House to the Secretary of State in accordance with the Rules of the House.

06/13/2008 – Read by title, adopted.

06/12/2008 – Scheduled for floor debate on 6/13/08.

06/11/2008 – Read by title, ordered engrossed, and passed to 3rd reading.

06/10/2008 – Reported favorably (12-0).

06/09/2008 – Read by title, under the rules, referred to the Committee on Education.

06/05/2008 – Read by title. Lies over under the rules.

HB 871 – 2008 Regular Session

03/31/2008 – Read by title, under the rules, referred to the Committee on Education.

03/21/2008 – First appeared in the Interim Calendar on 3/21/2008.

03/21/2008 – Under the rules, provisionally referred to the Committee on Education.

03/21/2008 – Pre filed.

Below is the history on a similar bill proposed thirteen years earlier. We were not the first to address this issue!

HB 132 – 1997 Regular Session

04/25/1997 – Tentatively scheduled to be heard on 4/30/1997 at 9 A.M. in Committee Room 1.

03/31/1997 – Read by title, rules suspended, under the rules, provisionally referred to the Committee on EDUCATION.

01/22/1997 – Under the rules, provisionally referred to the Committee on EDUCATION.

01/17/1997 – Pre filed.

Thank You

This experience reinforced for me the importance of selecting leaders who understand our values and concerns. I cannot imagine writing this without thanking some of the legislators who not only supported us consistently for three years with their votes, but who also spoke up for us and helped us pass this legislation. May God bless them, and make them to prosper.

Representative Cameron Henry
Senator Conrad Appel
Representative Frank Hoffmann
Representative John LaBruzzo
Representative Brett Geymann
Representative Fred Mills
Representative John Schroder
Senator Mike Walsworth
Senator Ann Duplessis
Representative Thomas Carmody
Representative Hollis Downs
Representative Jonathan Perry
Representative Walker Hines
Representative M. J. Smiley
Representative Henry Burns
Senator A.G. Crowe
Senator Jack Donahue
Senator Dale Erdey
Senator John Smith

This experience has also helped me understand the importance of having the right person in the Governor's office. I believe Governor Jindal understands the concerns that are important to us as parents. May the Lord bless his family and the Louisiana families he serves!

The author, Lisa Arceri, can be contacted by email at lisaarceri@ yahoo.com.